The Anti-Bubbles

The Anti-Bubbles

Opportunities Heading into Lehman Squared and Gold's Perfect Storm

Diego Parrilla

BUSINESS EXPERT PRESS

The Anti-Bubbles: Opportunities Heading into Lehman Squared and Gold's Perfect Storm

First published in 2017 by
Business Expert Press, LLC
222 East 46th Street, New York, NY 10017
www.businessexpertpress.com

ISBN-13: 978-1-63157-982-0 (paperback)
ISBN-13: 978-1-63157-983-7 (e-book)

Business Expert Press Finance and Financial Management Collection

Collection ISSN: 2331-0049 (print)
Collection ISSN: 2331-0057 (electronic)

Cover and interior design by Exeter Premedia Services Private Ltd., Chennai, India

First edition: 2017

10 9 8 7 6 5 4 3 2 1

Printed in the United States of America.

To my wife, Gema, and my children, Yago, Lucas, and Carmen,
who bless my life.

To my parents, Paco and Nieves, my inspiration and role models.

To my sisters, Nieves and Marta, the geniuses of the family.

And of course, to my sister Belén and my brother Paco, my guardian angels.

Abstract

The Anti-Bubbles is a forward-looking analysis of the opportunities, risks, and unintended consequences of testing the limits of monetary policy, testing the limits of credit markets, and testing the limits of fiat currencies.

The Anti-Bubbles is a contrarian framework that challenges the status quo and complacency of Global Markets toward the Central Bank Put, the false belief and misconception that Central Banks and Governments are infallible and in full control.

The Anti-Bubbles presents the "Lehman Squared" and "Gold's Perfect Storm" investment theses, elaborating on the front page article published in the Financial Times written edition on the 8th August, 2016 called "Gold's Perfect Storm."

Similar to the authors' first book *The Energy World is Flat: Opportunities from the end of Peak Oil*, the "the Anti-Bubbles" makes extensive use of historical and interdisciplinary analogies, and coins innovative ideas and concepts such as "anti-bubbles," "the acronyms," or "monetary super-cycle" among others, which have the potential to become mainstream concepts over the next few years.

The Anti-Bubbles presents both sides of the story, including a "premortem analysis" and powerful theories such as Larry Summer's prudent imprudence of fiscal expansions, George Soros' reflexivity theory applied to monetary policy, or Mohamed El-Erian's T-junction and diplomatic neutrality, among others.

Finally, the book presents a practical implementation guide on "how to make money from the anti-bubbles" (gold, volatility, and correlation) and debunks a number of common implementation mistakes, such as the debate between gold versus gold equities and physical versus paper. In addition to a practical implementation guide on how to avoid the bubbles (duration, government bonds, credit, high yield, emerging markets, and equities) identifying the hidden risks of volatility, false correlation, liquidity, and leverage, that may lead to a "Lehman Squared" scenario.

Keywords

bubbles: duration bubble, financial bubble, Lehman crisis, Lehman 1.0, Lehman squared, anti-bubbles: correlation, gold, liquidity, volatility, tail risk, monetary policy: acronyms, LTRO, negative interest rates, no limits, QE, QQE, test limits of monetary policy, fiscal policy, prudent, imprudence, test limits of credit markets, central bank put, diplomatic neutrality, false correlation, fiat currencies, gold's perfect storm, Gresham's Law, monetary supercycle, paper money, Reflexivity Theory, test limits of fiat currencies, T-junction, Chinese yuan CNY, euro, gold derivatives, gold equities, gold options, gold insurance, Japanese yen JPY, paper gold, physical gold, precious metals, relative value, smart gold, U.S. dollar

Contents

Quotations from the book

"From Risk-Free Interest to Interest-Free Risk."

"Bubbles and anti-bubbles represent a distorted view of the world—artificially inflated and artificially deflated valuations respectively—supported by misconceptions. In that sense, anti-bubbles provide investors with an effective defense against bubbles, just like anti-viruses protect against viruses, or anti-missiles protect against missiles."

—Diego Parrilla

Blurbs endorsing "The Anti-bubbles"

"Sound money is coming, like it or not. There is a new dawn for gold as a wealth preservation tool and the anti-bubble thesis and the "smart gold" strategy outlined by Diego Parrilla are worth reading. The illusion of growth by central planning is over. Time to prepare. Anti-Bubble."

—Daniel Lacalle, Fund Manager and Best-Selling Author

"Diego is one of the most original thinkers in the industry. His thesis for The Energy World is Flat literally changed my entire framework on oil, and commodities in general. The Anti-Bubbles is equally profound and equally important."

—Raoul Pal, Author, Global Macro Investor Newsletter

"Anti-Bubbles" is a very timely and succinct book describing, in terms anyone can understand, how the world's central banks have totally warped the world's financial markets on an epic scale. When this bubble, that the central banks created, unwinds it will impact everyone and everything, just as 2008 did, only differently. Read this book to get prepared."

—Bill Fleckenstein, Chief Investment Officer Fleckenstein Capital

"As the world lurches from one dangerous, central bank-engineered bubble to the next, the stakes are raised each time. Diego does a masterful job of not only explaining how reckless monetary policy and credit expansion are setting the world on course for disaster, but also identifies solutions that can help investors protect their wealth and take advantage of the opportunities ahead of the upcoming crisis."

—Grant Williams, Co-Founder of Real Vision Television

Foreword by Daniel Lacalle

The Dawn of a New Age

In the past 50 years, the world has seen more than 150 financial crises. The indiscriminate creation of money without support from savings or goods and services lies behind each and every one of those events.

The only policy that has existed since then has been to "solve" each crisis with the same method, lowering interest rates and increasing money supply. However, the diminishing returns are evident.

We cannot deny the importance of the past 50 years in the creation of prosperity and reducing poverty, but we must be aware of the growing imbalances of the world economy. Debt at historical highs, tax burden at record levels all over the OECD, and a surprising new outcome to the inflationary policies conducted by central banks: disinflation. Secular stagnation is something that the monetarists and MIT inflation advocates could not expect. Massive increases in money supply and a currency war that has reached unprecedented levels have created the opposite effect of what central planners had desired: low interest rates, low growth, and low inflation.

Investors find themselves in a conundrum, because we see a massive level of inflation in financial asset prices, equities, and bonds in particular, but very little fundamental rationale behind the multiples and yields of those assets.

Financial repression, that is artificially manipulating the price and quantity of money by lowering interest rates and currency devaluation continues to create and inflate bubbles that have the potential of generating another crisis in the near future. But the difficulty, for investors and economists, is to understand and time when those bubbles will burst.

Financial repression does something else. By lowering rates and devaluing, it clouds the perception of risk and investors take more and more of it in exchange for some yield. This race to the edge of the cliff is best exemplified by the fact that junk bonds are today trading at the lowest yield seen in more than 35 years. Investors are desperately trying to shield portfolios from negative interest rates and lower value of money, and in doing so they are centrally forced to take levels of risks that the same investors would have considered unacceptable 10 years ago.

Financial crises never happen in those assets or areas of the economy that we deem as risky. They always brew in those parts of the economy that we consider safe, almost bullet-proof. Housing was a clear example. Infrastructure is another. Oil, as Diego Parrilla and I explained in "The Energy World Is Flat," was another one. The misperception of supply and the exaggeration of potential demand contribute to making bubbles rational, even defended by so-called experts. Today the risks are clear in the unprecedented amount of negative yielding bonds and the explosive combination of high multiples with poor earnings in equities.

We, as economists and investors, have yet to find a comprehensive and rigorous analytical process to understand bubbles and, more importantly, their peak. This will be difficult, since most of the academia and analysts defend central planning and ignore—even deny—the problem of financial bubbles. When the thesis starts from the premise that the government will be able to divert the course of economic cycles, the conclusion is going to be inevitably flawed.

Therefore, we cannot count on mainstream economics to undertake a serious analysis of the creation, burst and implications of bubbles. I recommend our readers to search online or on scholar articles for papers on financial bubbles. For something that has caused so much distress in the world economy, it will be surprising for our readers to find out how little has been written about this phenomenon and, more importantly, how weak the conclusions and recommendations are. The problem is almost always ascribed to lack of regulation or insufficient central planning.

Is it not curious? How can more regulation eliminate the risk of artificially low rates and excess liquidity created by central planners? Do we really believe that more quantitative easing and central planning will solve the problems created by the same policies?

There is an alternative way of approaching the imminent burst of the latest bubble. The Anti-Bubble, that Diego Parrilla explains in this book.

In a world where excess liquidity becomes the norm and a rise of interest rates from 0 to 0.25 percent can cause shockwaves in the markets, it is essential to understand optionality, hedging and the investment that will help mitigate the inevitable losses that can be caused by excess tolerance for risk.

Even if we believe that we are not taking excessive risk, we might be blinded by a decade of disguising imbalances with money supply. The United States created more money in the 8 years of the Obama administration than in all its previous history as a sovereign nation.

We all have seen in the previous financial crises that even the most conservative construction of portfolios is damaged dramatically when the system comes into question. That happened due to a small part of the economy, housing. Now imagine for a second if the entire monetary system collapses due to the effects of years of excess.

The reader might disagree with some of the premises and estimates of this book, but there is something that no one can question, because it is irrefutable. It is extremely easy to create a financial bubble, but the burst and its side effects are becoming more and more difficult to overcome, and we are exiting every financial crisis with more debt and less growth than the previous one. As such, this book provides an excellent framework to understand the new paradigm for gold, options, hedging of positions, and the protection of wealth.

Sound money is coming, like it or not. There is a new dawn for gold as a wealth preservation tool and the "smart gold" strategy outlined by Diego Parrilla as well as his anti-bubble thesis is something that is worth reading.

The illusion of growth by central planning is over. Time to prepare. Anti-Bubble.

Daniel Lacalle is a PhD, Economist, Fund Manager, Professor of Global Economy, and author of "Life In The Financial Markets," "Escape from the Central Bank Trap" and "The Energy World Is Flat" (with Diego Parrilla).

About the Structure of the book

The Anti-Bubbles: Opportunities heading into Lehman Squared and Gold's Perfect Storm is a contrarian framework that challenges the complacency of global markets as Central Banks, Governments, and Market Participants continue to inflate the largest financial bubble in history.

I have coined the concept of *anti-bubble* with a double meaning and objective.

First, an anti-bubble describes the process by which asset valuations are artificially ***deflated***, in stark contrast to traditional financial bubbles, the process by which asset valuations are artificially ***inflated***. In other words, anti-bubbles described are the exact opposite, the inverse, of traditional financial bubbles.

Second, an anti-bubble describes a defense mechanism against bubbles, just like an antimissile may be a valuable defense against missiles.

Based on this simple idea, this book presents a *contrarian* forward-looking framework that I hope will help investors identify the bubbles and anti-bubbles in the system so they can, first and foremost, avoid the enormous risks they may be inadvertently taking, and second, take advantage of the opportunities these misconceptions create.

Whilst the exact timing is unknown, and it may be a long time before the bubbles eventually burst and the anti-bubbles reprice sharply higher, but this process is in my view "a matter of when, not a matter of if." The exact timing is unknown, but there are plenty of catalysts that could trigger and accelerate very sudden and violent market moves, so we should better prepare.

I believe that we are already in the *twilight phase*, where the *false-beliefs* that have artificially inflated and deflated bubbles and anti-bubbles are starting to be challenged and will eventually be proven to be misconceptions.

The Flattening of the Energy World Investment Thesis

I am very familiar with contrarian frameworks.

Early 2014, crude oil was comfortable trading above $110/bbl when, together with my co-author Daniel Lacalle, I finished writing my first book: *The Energy World is Flat: Opportunities from the end of Peak Oil*, a transformational framework that challenged many core fundamental beliefs prevailing in the energy market at the time.

The collapse of crude oil prices, the end of crude oil's monopoly in transportation demand, the end of the Organization of the Petroleum Exporting Countries (OPEC)'s oligopoly, the collapse in liquefied natural gas (LNG) prices, the emergence of a natural gas glut, the emergence of the "energy broadband" (a term we coined to describe the global network of land and "floating pipelines" in the form of LNG infrastructure), were among some of our contrarian and controversial views.

Quotes such as "the last barrel of oil will be worth zero, not millions" sounded like science fiction to many people at the time. Not anymore.

The chapter "the Btu that broke OPEC's back" (an adaptation of "the straw that broke the camel's back") challenged the belief that the "Central Bank of Oil" was in full control, and described how the transformational framework was leading to a highly unstable equilibrium.

The timing was very uncertain, but in our view "a matter of when, not a matter of if."

It only took a few months for some of those misconceptions to abruptly disappear. On November 29, 2014, a few months after my book was published, Saudi Arabia surprised the world "letting market forces determine the price," proving some beliefs to be misconceptions, and leading to a sharp and painful correction across energy and global markets.

To our credit, the contrarian framework and investment thesis of the *Flattening of the Energy World* we presented in our book has not only survived the passage of time, but it has also been reinforced. Today, there is a better understanding and wider acceptance of the relentless power of technology, the battle for supply, the battle for demand, and many other factors that in our view would contribute to a *Flatter Energy World* with abundant, cheaper, cleaner, and more reliable energy.

The transformational framework has disrupted global and energy markets, producing major winners and losers in the process, and still continues today. As Heraclito reminded us, "the only permanent thing in life is change."

Lehman Squared and Gold's Perfect Storm Investment Thesis

The contrarian framework and investment thesis of this book are as controversial—if not more—than the *Flattening of the Energy World* was at the time of publishing in 2014.

As of writing, the markets remain very complacent with *monetary expansion without limits* and *credit expansion without limits*, the two "magic wands" that Central Banks and Governments are using every time they face a crisis and/or unsatisfactory growth.

As a result, the markets continue to inflate the greatest financial bubble in history: a wave of *parallel synchronous bubbles* across government bonds, duration, credit, high yield, emerging markets, and equities, based on the belief (in my view misconception) that Central Banks are infallible and in full control and will always be able and willing to step-in and protect investors.

There are clear parallels between my two books. The bubble in energy markets was partially fueled by the complacent belief (now confirmed misconception) that OPEC (the "Central Bank of Oil") was infallible and in full control. Today, the bubbles across current markets are partially fueled by the complacent belief that Central Banks are infallible and in full control. Wishful thinking. Time will tell.

Structure of the Book

There are also clear parallels between the structure of my first book *The Energy World is Flat* and *The Anti-Bubbles*.

Both books follow a *deductive* structure, presenting the concepts and ideas first and the conclusions and implementation recommendations later.

The first sections of the book present key concepts such as the "Anti-Bubbles," the investment thesis of "Lehman Squared" and "Gold's

Perfect Storm," which are analyzed and broken down into their main building blocks: First, "testing the limits of monetary policy," which is leading to the greatest bubble in duration in history. Second, "testing the limits of credit markets" driven by the "desperate search for yield." And third, "testing the limits of fiat currencies," which describes the reset of the system and the monetary supercycle in gold prices.

Quotes such as "gold has a few hundred dollars of downside and a few thousand dollars of upside" may sound like science fiction to many people, and will remind the readers of the first book of our provocative quotes such as "the last barrel of oil won't be worth millions... It will be worth zero." Time will tell.

In the meantime, I hope the ideas and framework of this book will become a helpful roadmap to avoid the extraordinary risks and opportunities ahead of us.

Good luck and enjoy the reading!

CHAPTER 1

Bubbles and Anti-bubbles

Market bubbles don't grow out of thin air.
They have a solid basis in reality,
but a reality distorted by a misconception.

—George Soros

The Greatest Bubble in History

On June 5, 2014, following in the footsteps of the Scandinavian Central Banks, the European Central Bank (ECB) became the first major monetary authority to introduce negative interest rates, smashing the limits of the almighty Zero Interest Rate Policy (ZIRP) and perpetuating the monetary snowball inflating the greatest financial bubble in history.

My head was spinning. A reduction from zero to –0.1 percent was arguably small, but for me was a game-changer, a quantum leap from the years of controversial *unconventional* monetary policies of zero interest rates. A step too far into the unchartered territory of monetary experiments *without limits*.

"Mario Draghi has broken the floor in interest rates. Time to rewrite the rules of finance and asset valuations" I told myself, as my engineering mind prompted nerdy analogies such as "Mario has just broken the upper boundary speed of light. Time to rewrite Einstein's Relativity Theory" and "Mario has just broken the lower boundary of zero Kelvin. Time to rewrite the laws of Thermodynamics."

To me, the implications were *that* enormous.

The ECB announcement was a "Fukushima moment" for me, a sudden realization that something truly major had just happened.

"At 2.46 pm on the 11th of March 2011, the largest earthquake in the history of Japan triggered a giant tsunami wave that would change the energy world forever" read the opening lines of my first book, *The*

Energy World is Flat: Opportunities from the end of Peak Oil, which I had just finished cowriting at the time negative interest rates were introduced by the ECB announcement.

The parallel between both book openings is not a coincidence. Both books present contrarian frameworks inspired by *game changers* that challenge the status quo and complacency of the markets, at the time of writing.

The Energy World is Flat argued that "the collapse in crude oil prices was a matter of when, not a matter of if" and "the last barrel of oil won't be worth millions, it will be worth zero," ideas that were highly contrarian to the then prevailing beliefs, and sounded like science fiction at the time. Not anymore.

Some of the ideas of this book, such as "Lehman Squared," the "Monetary supercycle," or "Gold's Perfect Storm" may sound as crazy as the ideas and coined concepts of the energy book—when we first published them.

I belong to the school of "no-free-lunch economics" and caution against the complacency of the markets. Time will tell if my fears are unjustified and we can solve all problems by simply printing more money and borrowing more money. Wishful thinking in my humble view. Time will tell.

Testing the Limits of Monetary Policy

The ECB rate cut into negative interest rates was not a first. The experiment of negative interest rates had been in place in Scandinavia since 2009, but most people, myself included, agreed that these relatively small economies did not pose a threat to the financial stability of global markets per se, at least directly.

It turned out that the *Scandinavian experiment* was considered a success by some influential Central Bankers, including the president of the ECB, who eventually decided to adopt it, turning a local experiment into a global risk.

The decision had been telegraphed to the market via the media and analysts, but was nevertheless very controversial. Mario Draghi delivered the announcement with his usual conviction and decisiveness, reminding the historic and overwhelming success of his famous "We will do *whatever it takes* to save the Euro... and believe me, it will be enough," that earned him the nickname of "Super Mario" and the respect and fear of the markets. The motto "never fight the ECB" now carried as much weight and respect as the widely accepted "never fight the Fed."

In turn, the European experiment of negative interest rates was considered a success by other influential global policymakers, including Haruhiko Kuroda, the Governor of the Central Bank of Japan, who on January 29, 2016 surprised the market with the introduction of nominal negative interest rates for the first time in the history of Japan, the country that had been pushing the boundaries of monetary policy for decades. The *Japanese experiment* is in my view, without any doubt, one of the greatest financial time-bombs in the making.

But it is important to note that the recent wave of monetary incentives and experiments originated in the United States in 2008 when, in response to the Global Financial Crisis, the U.S. Federal Reserve, led by Ben Bernanke, cut interest rates to zero and printed unprecedented amounts of money to buy government bonds via a process known as Quantitative Easing (QE), opening a new era of unconventional monetary policies.

QE, put simply, is a process whereby *the left pocket* (the Central Bank) lends money to *the right pocket* (the Government). QE was highly controversial at first, and questioned the principle of Central Bank Independence and risks to inflation and financial stability, but was gradually accepted and eventually embraced with full force.

QE was conveniently positioned by Central Bankers as a *domestic* policy, but it had a direct impact on devaluation of the USD (and therefore the CNY via the peg) against the EUR and the JPY.

QE became the latest weapon in the *currency wars* that export deflation and problems to other economies. Without any doubt, the QE program by the U.S. Federal Reserve, and the subsequent devaluation of the USD and the CNY, had a direct major impact in the European Government crisis of the following years, which put the Euro near the brink of collapse in the summer of 2012.

Europe and Japan were forced to defend themselves and adopt aggressive unconventional monetary measures that would help counteract the aggression from the U.S. Federal Reserve. A vicious cycle of monetary easing that pushed Europe and Japan to adopt monetary policy "without limits," whereby the objective justified the means, sending interest rates into the unchartered territory of negative interest rates.

The implications were enormous. To start, negative interest rates broke the theoretical ceiling in bond prices, perpetuating the already exuberant bubble in fixed income.

Ever-increasing bond prices was a new paradigm that squeezed-out short speculative positions, squeezed-in underweight positions, and incentivized the speculation that is feeding the greatest bubble in government bonds in history, blessed by the complacency of the markets.

The epicenter of the problem is the artificial demand from Central Banks, which has incentivized—if not forced—investors to lend for longer and longer maturities in exchange of lower and lower yields, feeding the greatest bubble in *duration* in history.

Testing the Limits of Credit Markets

The duration bubble has created unprecedented problems for savers and investors, who in order to generate income, are incentivized—if not forced—to lend to weaker and weaker credits, and for longer and longer maturities, in exchange for lower and lower yields.

A "desperate search for yield" that behaves like a steamroller that crashes yields and inflates valuations across asset classes, starting by government bonds and spreading to risk assets such as credit markets.

The desperate search for yield applies to all borrowers. The demand for high-quality borrowers, known as high-grade, has pushed yields to historical low levels, which has once again incentivized—if not forced—investors to lend to weaker and weaker credits for longer and longer maturities.

The desperate search for yield has benefited the weakest borrowers the most, inflating parallel bubbles in high-yield credit and emerging markets, among others.

As a result, the desperate search for yield has inflated the entire capital structure, directly impacting not only the valuation of debt instruments, but also valuation of equity, adding yet another parallel bubble to the list.

The epicenter of all these parallel bubbles is the *belief* (in my view *misconception*) that Central Banks are infallible and in full control. The synchronous appreciation of all these markets creates a risk of synchronous depreciation as and when the belief is proven to be a misconception, which creates a risk of *false diversification*, as a portfolio composed of government bonds, high-grade credit, high-yield credit, emerging markets, and equities are just the exact same trade.

Testing the Limits of Fiat Currencies

Central Banks and Governments tend to respond to crisis with two simple and easy solutions: print more money and borrow more money.

These easy solutions seem to have worked well in previous crises, but the reality is that they do not resolve problems: they simply postpone and often enlarge them.

As a student of the school of "no free lunch economics," I worry about the current path and try to understand how and when the consequences of these excesses will manifest themselves.

We need to be mindful that while Central Banks and Governments may have already gone too far with their policies, it can get much worse as they will do "whatever it takes" to keep the wheels spinning. A double-up, triple-up, and quadruple-up of bets that are enlarging, not resolving, the problems.

Monetary policy and fiat currencies are two sides of the same coin. As Central Bankers know well, during the gold standard they could not print gold to control the monetary base or interest rates. The global system was much more rigid, which has its pros and cons.

And with great power comes great responsibility, goes the saying, and why Voltaire claimed that "paper currencies eventually converge to their intrinsic value: paper." A reflection that giving Central Banks and Government the power to "print their way out of a problem" is a slippery slope. A path that will ultimately result in a loss of confidence in the currencies and institutions that created them. A process of competitive devaluations that does not solve problems and that will conclude in a "monetary supercycle" leading major winners and losers in the process, as we will discuss later in the book.

Exuberance versus Complacency

Financial bubbles are often associated with *exuberant* market behavior, a sense of *excess* and *market craze* that drives a surge in asset prices unwarranted by the fundamentals.

As a corollary, any apparent lack of exuberance can be misunderstood as a *new paradigm*, as it gives the perception of stable equilibrium, instead of the unstable equilibrium that characterizes bubbles.

Indeed, I believe the most dangerous bubbles are driven by *complacency*, a sense of *conformism* that makes us believe that unstable equilibriums are stable.

The crude oil bubble, for example, was inflated by complacency that OPEC was in full control or that crude oil could maintain its monopoly in transportation unchallenged forever.

I believe the parallel monetary bubbles are being inflated by complacency too. Complacency with monetary policy without limits, complacency with credit expansion and fiscal policies without limits, complacency with the desperate search for yield, and the parallel bubbles in government bonds, duration, credit, equity, but also complacency that Central Banks can keep volatility artificially low, exposing hidden risks in correlation and liquidity. These dynamics are closely interlinked and could lead to a chain reaction where if any of the previous bubbles is exposed and bursts, it will most likely expose and burst the others too.

Central Banks are aware of these risks, which explains their obsession with stability and low realized volatility. A dynamic that feeds the beast called complacency, because it rewards bad behavior and encourages speculation. A dangerous unstable equilibrium.

Beliefs versus Misconceptions

As George Soros famously said:

> Financial markets, far from accurately reflect all the available knowledge; always provide a distorted view of reality. The degree of distortion may vary from time to time. Sometimes it is quite insignificant, at other times, it is quite pronounced. Sometimes, market expectations eventually become so far removed from reality that people are forced to recognize that a *misconception* is involved.

In *The Energy World is Flat*, my co-author and I challenged a number of beliefs (in our view misconceptions) such as the Peak Oil theory, the belief that OPEC was infallible and in full control, or the belief that crude oil could maintain a monopoly in transportation demand unchallenged, among many others. Some of those beliefs are now confirmed as misconceptions. Some are still in the *twilight zone*.

Under the new regime, old beliefs become misconceptions. The *Flattening of the Energy World* described a new regime driven by transformational and disruptive technological processes, "game changers," such as fracking, which set a before and after.

The process from belief to misconception tends to be gradual and creates a twilight period where beliefs and misconceptions coexist. Market opinions tend to be very divided and often give way to highly polarized views, as it is the case today.

The only persistent thing in life is change.

—Heraclitus

This process tends to reach a tipping point when the rate of conversion accelerates, potentially quite drastically, leading to large sudden dislocations in the markets.

Stable, Unstable, and Metastable Equilibriums

The complacency of financial markets can also be explained in terms of physics.

In physics, we define *stable equilibrium* as "a state in which a body tends to return to its original position after being disturbed." Visually, we can think of a marble inside a large bowl. Once displaced from its stable equilibrium at the bottom center, the marble will gyrate around the inside walls of the bowl but will eventually settle in the original position as illustrated in Figure 1.1.

The exact opposite dynamic is known as *unstable equilibrium*, "a state in which a body that is slightly displaced will depart further from the original position." Visually, we can think of a marble on top of an upside-down bowl. Once displaced from its unstable equilibrium at the top,

Figure 1.1 Stable equilibrium

Figure 1.2 Unstable equilibrium

Figure 1.3 Metastable equilibrium

the marble will move down the outside surface of the bowl further and further away from the original position as illustrated in Figure 1.2.

Somewhere in between, and very important in the real world, there is a dynamic known as *metastable equilibrium*, which is defined as "a state in which a body tends to return to its original position after being disturbed up to a break-even point, but that will move further away from the original position after being disturbed beyond that break-even point." The marble inside the bowl looks like a *stable equilibrium*, but in practice is a *metastable equilibrium*, similar to a bowling pin, which will wobble back to equilibrium for small disturbances but will tip over for larger disturbances as illustrated in Figure 1.3.

Optically stable equilibriums may hide the danger of metastable equilibriums as illustrated in Figure 1.4. This is not only true in physicals but

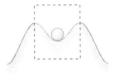

Figure 1.4 Unchartered territories. Optically stable, but may be metastable

also in financial markets. The Energy World is Flat and the Anti-Bubbles challenge complacent beliefs in stable equilibriums, that in reality may turn out to be misconceptions, as the real market dynamics are governed by metastable equilibriums. There are two main reasons why our judgment may be blurred.

First, we need to understand the physical limits of the bowl. They often tend to extrapolate the observed shape and material of the bowl beyond what we have observed. Empirically, we could "test the limits of our bowl" by gradually increasing the distortion to the marble. Our observations may show that the marble reverts to its original position, indicating a possible stable equilibrium. But as Karl Popper famously taught us, "one million positive observations do not prove a theory true, but one single negative observation proves a theory wrong." We should be careful when extrapolating the results into the unknown. It would be naïve to assume the bowl—or monetary policy or credit markets, for that matter—have no limits.

Second, we need to understand that the bowl is dynamic. The assumption that the bowl is static over time is naïve. As Heraclitus taught us, "the only permanent thing in life is change."

One of the key drivers of dynamic change is technology. Applied to financial markets, technology is proving to be a powerful deflationary force that allows us, not only to achieve "more with less," but also leads to "quantum leaps" and "new paradigms." In The Energy World is Flat, some of the beliefs widely held by the market such as "OPEC is in full control," were challenged by technological changes such as shale and fracking. Those who push the marble ignoring the changes in the size of the bowl saw their marble crashing to the floor.

Another key driver of dynamic change is regulation, "the visible hand of the market." Beyond the well-intended policy measures introduced by

Governments and Central Banks, there are many more obscure unintended consequences of second and third order that may spin the marble out of control. In that sense, the Anti-Bubbles presents a framework where testing the limits of monetary policies and testing the limits of credit markets will eventually test the limits of fiat currencies. Indeed, the complacency of global markets and the desperate search for yield are testing the limits of a dynamic bowl into unchartered territory.

The OPEC Put

The belief that OPEC was in full control gave a false sense of security to many participants, who were counting on the ability and willingness of Saudi Arabia to cut production as and when necessary to preserve high oil prices. A dynamic known as the "OPEC floor" or the "OPEC put."

> *The Btu that broke OPEC's back.*
> *The collapse of crude oil prices*
> *is a matter of when, not a matter of if.*
>
> —*The Energy World is Flat*

The Energy World is Flat argued the transformational changes were creating a highly unstable equilibrium. From a fiscal perspective, at $100/bbl producers needed 1 barrel of oil to generate $100 of revenue. At $50/bbl they needed 2 barrels. And at $25/bbl they needed 4 barrels. That is, ceteris paribus, the lower the oil price the greater the volume they needed to produce. The exact opposite of what the markets believe at the time due to the complacency and misconception around OPEC's ability and willingness to cut production. Lower production at lower prices is a "double whammy" and creates a highly unstable equilibrium, which can be maintained for a while, but not forever.

The relentless flattening power of technology and the *battle for demand*, we argued, would exacerbate the *battle for supply*, leading to *more* oil production, not less, to generate the revenues they needed.

The misconception around OPEC's infallibility was debunked abruptly on November 29, 2014 when Saudi Arabia decided to "let the market forces decide the price." The collapse in prices validated the views we had presented in a chapter titled "The Btu that broke OPEC's back" (in clear reference to the straw that broke the camel's back).

The complacency around high oil prices incentivized the development of high marginal cost fields, such as ultradeep oil in Brazil or heavy crude oils in Venezuela and Canada, projects that have become very challenged due to the threats from the *battle for supply* (civil war between oil producers) and the *battle for demand* (whereby crude oil is increasingly competing for transportation demand with other alternative fuels such as natural gas, electric cars, and many other challengers).

Misconceptions can last for a long time. And the longer they persist, the more entrenched they become, and the more complacent the market becomes about them. Very dangerous.

The Central Bank Put

There are clear parallelisms between the OPEC put and the Central Bank put, the current complacent belief that Central Banks are in full control and will continue to successfully step-in and stabilize the markets as and when required.

> *Central Banks have become investors' best friends,*
> *but their instruments are limited. Central Bank bridging*
> *is far from a riskless and costless exercise.*
> —Mohamed El-Erian

The belief that the U.S. Federal Reserve (Fed) is infallible has been strengthened with every successful intervention, and has led to the common saying "never fight the Fed."

The ECB joined the monetary party somewhat late, but very decisively. Since his appointment, Mario Draghi has gained a status of invincibility. His "whatever it takes to save the Euro" will go down in history as one of the most epic battles won by a Central Banker.

The Bank of Japan (BOJ) enjoys mixed respect from the markets, and has seen some measures backfire spectacularly, such as the rally in the Yen after the introduction of negative interest rates. The BOJ has been forced to step into the markets and intervene on a regular basis, not only via the

Foreign Exchange (FX) channel, but also buying equities and other asset classes. A very slippery slope.

The People's Bank of China (PBOC) is in a similar situation to the BOJ, as they have been forced to intervene aggressively on numerous occasions. So far they have been able to contain the attacks, but the doubts are growing. The peg of the CNY to the USD has been a major source of imbalances, yet to be resolved.

The Swiss National Bank (SNB) went through one of the most spectacular fiascos in recent memory when on January 15, 2015 abandoned the 1.20 floor versus the Euro, creating mayhem in the currency markets. The shocking part of the SNB debacle was that they had—literally—infinite bullets in the form of printing their own currency.

The SNB fiasco is in stark contrast to other notorious Central Bank failures, such as the Bank of England (BOE), where interventions required selling of their finite foreign reserves. A lesson learnt by many investors, and a warning sign to those believing that the Central Banks are in full control.

The Anti-bubbles

I have coined the concept of *anti-bubble* with a double meaning and objective.

First, an anti-bubble describes the process by which asset valuations are artificially *deflated*, in stark contrast to traditional financial bubbles, the process by which asset valuations are artificially *inflated*. In other words, anti-bubbles described are the exact opposite, the inverse, of traditional financial bubbles.

Second, an anti-bubble describes a defense mechanism against bubbles, just like an antimissile may be a valuable defense against missiles.

Anti-bubbles are valued artificially low and will reflate—potentially quite suddenly and sharply—once the misconceptions that are artificially compressing them disappear.

Imagine, for example, a new treatment or medicine that is believed to dramatically improve the cure for a dangerous disease. The new treatment may not be totally proven yet, but the market tends to be quick and price-in higher valuations to the winners and price-in lower valuations to the losers.

There are two main scenarios here.

On the one hand, a scenario where the new treatment is proven true. it works and creates a new paradigm, a better world, where the old treatment is likely to become obsolete and eventually disappear.

On the other hand, a scenario where the new treatment does not work. The positive expectations that had been built-in in the winners turn out to be bubbles and quickly reprice lower, whilst—simultaneously— the negative expectations that had been built in the losers turn out to be anti-bubbles and quickly reprice higher.

There are several anti-bubbles in the current markets. The main three in my view are gold, volatility, and correlation, which can play an important dual role as "value investments" and portfolio diversifiers and portfolio insurance during "hostile markets," when investors need those returns the most.

In that sense, the anti-bubbles can be viewed as *antidotes* to protect against the risks in other parts of the portfolio, such as fixed income, credit, or equities.

Gold, the Anti-Bubble

From the highs of 2012 to the lows of December 2015, gold collapsed by almost 50 percent and the gold miners by almost 80 percent, leaving a sour taste to investors. The collapse in gold prices coincided with the surge of other asset classes (government bonds, high yield, emerging markets, credit, and equity).

The massive divergence in prices was not a coincidence. It was the result of the exact same factors: deflationary forces, monetary policy without limits, yield-seeking strategies, the Central Bank put, speculative flows, are some of the factors that have simultaneously inflated the bubbles and deflated the anti-bubbles.

Many investors had bought gold as an inflation hedge. Why hold gold if there is no threat of inflation? Worse, why hold gold if the threat is deflation?

Many investors had bought gold as a safe haven. Why hold gold if the Central Banks are infallible and in full control? Indeed, the "risk on" mentality supported allocations to riskier asset classes, such as equities and bonds.

The perception of infallibility of Central Banks has been self-reinforced through the build up of the bubble, reinforcing a (false, in my view) sense of security to investors. Every time the Central Banks have successfully intervened (both quantitatively and qualitatively) to support the market, the belief is strengthened and the wrong behavior rewarded, and incentivized. The Central Bank Put incentivizes strategies that "buy the dip," as any corrections are seen as opportunities to buy. In a way, "the Central Bank has my back," they think. And it has worked very well for a long time.

It is ironic and illustrative how the markets reacted to economic data over the past few years. Bad economic data was interpreted by the markets as a clear indication that Central Banks would step-in to protect investors with additional monetary incentives and stimuli, whilst the inverse was also true. As a result, the markets rallied on bad data and sold-off on good economic data. An upside down world and not a very healthy market dynamic, in my view.

Many investors joined the duration bubble and desperate search for yield. Whey hold gold if gold pays no yield? Worse, it has a negative carry?

All these beliefs will eventually become misconceptions, in my view, and lead to a sharp increase in gold prices.

I don't have a specific target for gold prices but like to say that the outlook is very asymmetric, offering "a few hundred dollars of downside and a few thousand dollars of upside." Similar to my contrarian views in energy, I believe much higher gold prices are "a matter of when, not a matter of if."

Volatility, the Anti-bubble

From the highs in implied and realized volatility during the Lehman crisis, implied volatility has been steadily trending lower and, at the time of writing, is trading at historical lows across many markets.

The ultra-low levels of implied volatility is consistent with the complacency and perception of low risk.

My view is totally the opposite and I believe the low levels of implied volatility not only hide huge risks but are also feeding even greater risks via dangerous structural leverage. A time bomb and the key Achilles' heel of global markets,

There are two main processes feeding the collapse in implied volatility. First, the Central Bank put, as described earlier.

Second, the complacent desperate search for yield, which incentivises investors to sell options and implied volatility. Indeed, investors have been large sellers of options in every shape and form. Investors that were long equities sold covered calls. Those who were not long, sold puts (so they could get long in case the puts were exercised).

And in large size and with significant leverage. Private banks have been offering structured products that monetize volatility and correlation plays, such as worst-of-baskets and other creative ideas that work very well... until they don't. These structures tend to be very highly leveraged and have the potential to wipe out the entire investment.

The monetization of volatility pushed implieds lower and lower and lower as a result of imbalances in supply and demand, which contributed to the self-fulfilling prophecy. An unstable equilibrium, which can reverse quite suddenly and violently. Dangerous.

A normalization of volatility is likely to result in an overshooting to the upside. That is, implied volatility will go much higher than its fair value or equilibrium level, whichever it ends up being.

Many quantitative models, such as Value at Risk (V@R) use realized and implied volatility to measure risk. As a result, artificially low levels of volatility can give a perception that the risk is lower than it actually is, which is likely to result in larger positions than the real risk would warrant. A time bomb.

Correlation, the Anti-bubble

The parallel bubbles across government bonds, credit, and equity markets hide another important risk: what goes up together may also fall down together.

Indeed, I expect the correlation between asset classes to polarize during periods of stress: financial assets will either be strongly positively correlated (go up and down together) or be strongly negatively correlated (when one goes up the other one goes down, and vice-versa). Those investors who naively expect normal correlations to hold during periods of stress may be in for a nasty surprise.

The quantitative models, such as Value at Risk (V@R) that use realized correlations as inputs, contribute to this problem of overconfidence and false diversification as they give the perception that portfolios are more diversified than they actually are. False diversification is a major hidden risk and time bomb for global markets, but also a major source of opportunity for those who know how to monetize them.

The fundamentals behind these risks set the foundation to the "Lehman Squared" and the "Gold Perfect Storm" investment theses that I will discuss in full detail in the following chapters.

The last sections of the book provide a practical guide on how investors can avoid the bubbles and take advantage of the anti-bubbles (gold, volatility, and correlation) as both value investments and portfolio insurance.

CHAPTER 2

Lehman Squared

Markets are constantly in a state of uncertainty and flux and money is made by discounting the obvious and betting on the unexpected.

—George Soros

West Side Story and Romeo and Juliet

"Feels like watching *West Side Story* when you've already seen *Romeo and Juliet*. Two stories that at first sight may look totally unrelated but to me are, in essence, the same story." That is how I feel about the Global Financial Crisis that shocked the world in 2008, which I call "Lehman 1.0" and the next crisis ahead, which I call "Lehman Squared."

Most people are quick to rightfully point at the differences. "Diego, one of the stories takes place in Italy, the other one in New York City. One took place centuries ago, and the other one just a few decades ago. One confronts two noble families, and the other one two gangs. How can this be the same story?" they argue.

To me, beyond the surface, the essence, whereby girl and boy from enemy groups fall in love, and live an impossible love story, complicated by the death of her brother by the boy in question, and the drama and dynamics around it are virtually an identical plot.

To, beyond the surface, the essence of the dynamics that led to the Global Financial Crisis of 2008 has clear similarities with today's global macroeconomic situation. We are dealing with extraordinarily complex and interrelated dynamics across economics, politics, and financial markets, most of which are not well enough understood even by market professionals, let alone non-professionals, which is why I will use a movie analogy, based on plots and principal characters that are easily understood. I will provide the more technical discussion and rationale for all these arguments throughout the rest of the book.

The goal of this exercise is to learn from past mistakes and try to anticipate and prevent future mistakes from happening. We can control our investment decisions. We cannot control the outcomes.

Remember, we are presenting a series of investment *thesis*, dynamic hypothesis based on assumptions, asymmetric probabilities and outcomes that are path dependent and change over time along with new information and events. Our investment thesis need to be validated, adapted, accepted, or rejected with new information. Therefore, my investment thesis should not be viewed as static frameworks or absolute truths, simply because they don't exist in the financial markets.

Lessons from Lehman 1.0

The Global Financial Crisis of 2008, also known as the Lehman crisis, caught most people by surprise. Today, with the benefit of hindsight, we have a very good understanding of our mistakes, some of which in my view we are repeating.

> *We will not have any more crashes in our time.*
> —John Maynard Keynes, 1927

Why Lehman Squared

I have called my investment thesis Lehman Squared for two simple reasons.

First, because the next crisis will be a "sequel" of the previous movie, I mean crisis.

Second, because the potential size and implications are much larger than for Lehman 1.0, and thus the "Squared" instead of Lehman 2.0.

A Premortem Analysis

With the benefit of hindsight, we have developed a very comprehensive "postmortem" analysis of the causes that led to Lehman 1.0. The goal is now to develop bridges of competence that will help us develop a "premortem" analysis of what the next global crisis may look like.

Let's review the plot and the principal characters of both movies, one by one.

The Miracle Technology

We love miracles. And we love technology. So, a movie with a miracle technology sounds promising. But, as we know, technologies tend to have two sides: a good side and a dark side.

Most of the policies that support robust economic growth in the long-run are outside of the province of the Central Bank.
—Ben Bernanke

Look at the nuclear technology for example. On the one hand, nuclear technology has played an important positive role in medicine and the generation of electricity, among others. On the other hand, however, nuclear has a dark side of nuclear accidents and bombs.

Or look at the Internet, another transformational technology. On the one hand, the Internet has transformed the way we communicate, learn, and live our lives. On the other hand, it has created challenges we did not have before, such as cybercrime or bad use and abuse of the Internet.

The Lehman 1.0 miracle technology was called securitization, another case of transformational technology with positive and negative applications. On the positive side, securitization has provided great benefits to both borrowers and lenders. On the negative side, viewed as a "miracle technology," securitization was pushed beyond its limits with massive volumes of all kinds of yield-seeking assets (including subprime mortgages) magically converted into tranches with credit ratings ranging from AAA-rated (risk-free) to "equity" (risky residue) that arbitraged the models and inputs. A miracle of alchemy that would transform lead or copper into gold.

The Lehman 1.0 *accident*, like in most action movies, was the result of a chain of parallel and sequential errors. With the benefit of hindsight, we can assign roles and characters to the key principal players.

The Greedy Arranger

One of the baddies of Lehman 1.0 were the investment banks that played the role of greedy arrangers. With the benefit of hindsight, it is obvious that the banks were conveniently arbitraging models and that the assumptions used by investment banks were flawed.

The banks also inadvertently played the role of *naive lender*, as they accumulated enormous risk on their balance sheet that they believed to be risk-free but turned out to be risky. A clear case of "believing their own... lies."

The Partner in Crime

Another key baddie of Lehman 1.0 were the rating agencies (in particular the main three, S&P, Moody's, and Fitch), which validated the process with theirs that gave credibility to the process and the rating agencies (playing the role of the "partner in crime") underestimated the risk of extreme events.

The Naive Lender

The role of the victim is played by the *naive lender*. Naive (trusted someone) is a kind generalization, as many lenders were simply *greedy* (tried to make some easy money) and *careless* (did not do their homework). In all cases, they conveniently believed the miracle of earning high spreads for lower credit risk.

The Greedy Borrower

The role of the greedy borrower during Lehman 1.0 was played by those who embarked in cheap debt beyond their limits. Many tried to plead ignorance, but all of them were trying to take advantage of the cheap and abundant credit.

At the extreme, unemployed people were taking mortgages to buy houses they could not afford. The result, the mortgage subprime (nice euphemism), which contributed to the bubble in the housing markets.

The Acronyms

The role of "weapon" by which the miracle technology does the damage is played by the "acronyms," instruments named by their initials that everyone used but few truly understood.

The acronyms of the Lehman 1.0. crisis were the ABS, CDO, CLO, and other more funky versions such as the synthetic CDO square, an obscure way to add leverage and risk.

Now, in simple terms, what does an acronym do? What is it, in a sense? Well, I like to define as a mechanism, a vehicle, by which "we lend a lot of money, to the wrong people, in the wrong size, at the wrong price, and arguably, at the wrong time." That's really what all those obscure instruments were doing: lending.

The Sleeping Policemen

The role of the "sleeping policeman" in Lehman 1.0 was played by the Central Bank and regulators. It was only with the benefit of hindsight that they realized the excesses and the lack of regulation. Despite the warnings, it is fair to say that central banks were genuinely caught by surprise.

Now, if you fast forward to where we are today, we can draw some clear parallels.

The New Miracle Technology

The role of miracle technology is played by monetary policy. Solving problems is as easy as cutting interest rates, printing money, and why not, tax people for holding that cash.

The role of miracle technology is also indirectly played via fiscal policy. The nonsense has reached an extreme that governments are now paid for borrowing (OMG), which incentivizes the wrong behavior (the more you borrow, the more interest you get paid). A dynamic that we will discuss in detail later, under the "prudent imprudence" chapter.

The New Acronyms

The role of the weapon is once again played by acronyms. In this case QE (Quantitative Easing), QQE (Quantiative and Qualitative Easing), LTRO (Long Term Repurchase Obligations), or YCC (Yield Curve Control), among others. What do they do? Very easy. They are "*lending* a lot of money, to the wrong people, in the wrong size, at the wrong price at the wrong time." Sounds familiar.

The New Partner in Crime

The role of the "partner in crime" (previously played by the rating agencies, which enabled and validated the acronyms) is now played by the Central Bank. Monetary policy without limits is incentivizing—or rather forcing—investors to lend for longer and longer and to weaker and weaker credits. A desperate effort to fight deflation, they argue, but that once again incentivizes the wrong behavior.

Who Polices the Police?

A twist of the current situation, deeply concerning to me, is that *supervision* is one of the key core competences of Central Banks. As a result, there seems to be a duality, a conflict, which makes me wonder *who polices the police*, or *quis custodiet ipsos custodes*, as they say in Latin.

In the movies, it is quite common to have policemen who looked like goodies but turned out to be baddies. Time will tell if Central Banks will go down in history as heroes or villains.

The New Greedy Arranger

The role of the greedy arranger played by the Investment Bank in the Lehman 1.0 crisis is unfortunately also played by the Central Bank, which is the one that is incentivizing volume. In this case, given the massive stakes, superheroes or supervillains.

In addition, there is also a role of passive arranger played by the Benchmarks that is contributing to the vicious cycle. Many institutional allocators have strategic allocations to bonds, which means they are expected to stay invested under neutral market conditions. In practical terms, it acts as a leash that is taking the institutional investors for a dangerous stroll around "bubble park."

Those allocators that have taken "underweight" positions have been penalized by underperformance as the bubbles carry on. A dynamic that has forced them to cut losses and go back to neutral. Some others, embracing the bubble, have gone overweight. The entry door is pretty large. The exit door probably not. Liquidity, as discussed, a major risk and consideration that is building in the system.

The New Naïve Borrower

The role of the greedy borrower is once again played by those borrowing beyond their limits. Governments are the greatest beneficiaries, as their cost of refinancing is dropping beyond the imaginable, at negative interest rates.

Corporates have been major beneficiaries of the monetary snowball and the credit steamroller, which is crushing borrowing costs beyond the imaginable. With the expansion of QE to high-grade credit, many corporates are now able to borrow at negative rates. Total nonsense in a ZIRP constrained world, but a new reality.

The greatest beneficiaries are however the weakest credits, such as high yield and emerging markets. The bull market has spurred also record issuance. A borrowing party.

Building Bubbles

History tells us that lending too much money, to the wrong people, at the wrong price is likely to end in speculation and bubbles.

During the Lehman 1.0. crisis, the wall of money went principally into real estate and fixed investments. It was large, but somewhat contained and channeled.

Unfortunately, this time around, the vast amounts of money that are flowing into government bonds, thanks to central banks' monetary policy without limits, is having a spillover effect into many, many more markets, in a much more global way, much more spread, and much bigger, which is, obviously, much harder to control.

The corollary of inflating synchronous bubbles is that they are also likely to deflate synchronously.

The Complacency Phase

I believe we are currently in the complacency phase of the bubble, supported by the belief that Central Banks are in full control. We have had some scares, such as the "taper tantrum" of September 2014, or the "CNY mini-devaluation crisis" of January 2015 following the first hike by the Federal Reserve, which have reinforced the perception of infallibility and control.

The normalization of monetary policy in the United States seems underway. The two consecutive hikes following the U.S. elections are a very important positive development for global markets in my opinion. They are a test to the resilience of global markets. The jury is still out.

The Twilight Phase

The recent scares have casted some doubts into many people, which is leading to a polarization of views across markets participants. Many others remain confident and bullish.

> *This is not the end. It is not even the beginning of the end. It is the end of the beginning.*
>
> —Winston Churchill

The Burst

Time will tell if this movie will end in disaster, like Lehman 1.0, or will have a happy ending. The future is path dependent, and recent developments such as Brexit or Trump's presidency complicate things further. This new phase is likely to add fuel to the fire and increase the bets through fiscal expansions.

The Scapegoats

The Lehman 1.0 crisis was followed by a phase of blame and punishment, primarily inflicted upon the Investment Banks.

The current dynamics are different. A growing problem of inequality is emerging from financial inflation, which benefits those with financial assets the most. So far, Central Banks are able to operative at will outside of the radar of blame. The blame for many of the problems is being pointed toward globalization, and the proposed answer is protectionism, as it has become evident in the United Kingdom and the United States with Brexit and the election of Trump.

	Description	Lehman 1.0	Lehman Squared
The plot: A miracle technology	Every technology has good and bad uses. Nuclear power vs. weapons.	Abuse SECURITIZATION: Alchemy of creating AAA tranches from Junk.	Abuse MONETARY POLICY: Print money and incentivize debt.
The weapon: The Acronyms	Vehicles that lend too much money, to the wrong people, at the wrong time, at the wrong price.	**ABS, CLO,** and **CDO,** Collateralized Loan and Debt Obligations, and so on.	**QE** and **QQE,** Quantitative and Qualitative Easing, **LTRO, YCC,** …
Partner in crime	Validate the "miracle"	Rating Agencies	Central Banks
Greedy arranger	Benefit from volume	Investment Bank	Central Banks (Monetary Policy)
Naïve lender	Complacent lender	Institutional Investors attracted by higher yield and credit	Duration and Credit bubble via negative rates and benchmarks
Greedy borrower	Take advantage of cheap credit to borrow beyond its means.	Investment Bank	Governments, Corporates
Sleeping policeman	Regulator and Supervisor of Financial Stability should have identified and avoided problem.	Central Bank (Supervision) caught by surprise in a framework of loose regulation.	CB plays dual role Greedy Arranger and Supervisor: "who polices the police"?
Bubble	Excess lending eventually results in gross misallocation of capital.	Housing Market and Infrastructure	Epicenter Government Bonds, but spread to High Yield, Emerging Markets, IG Credit, Equities, ….

A New Beginning

The end of the Lehman 1.0 movie was a period of extraordinary monetary expansion. The beginning of the movie we are still watching. The following chapters of the book will provide a more in-depth analysis of both the causes and potential paths ahead. There are great opportunities and challenges ahead, which will leave major winners and losers, but as always, whatever happens. A financial crisis will not be the end of the world. No matter how the tables turn, the sun will still come out in the morning.

Bridges of Competence

My brain seems to be wired in a way that creates connections, analogies, and parallels all the time. My colleagues and team members know this well, as I am known for making extensive use of sporting analogies during the morning and strategy meetings.

One of those connections was triggered by the Fukushima nuclear accident. A mental bridge that connected the divergence in global natural gas prices with the Internet bubble. A big bridge, I know, but an idea that stayed with me and eventually took form in my first book.

If you don't understand it well enough, you can't explain it well enough.

—Albert Einstein

I had read Thomas Friedman's "The World is Flat" in 2003. The dot.com bubble was still fresh in everyone's memory, and had left a sour taste to many, but Friedman's book opened a completely different perspective. An inspirational "post-mortem" analysis about the transformational process that had "Flattened the World," thanks to a game-changing technology (the Internet), thanks to the large growth in capacity that took place during the boom (which, among others, wired the oceans with broadband), and thanks to the bust of the bubble (which made the technology available in large capacity virtually for free).

As I tried to explain the technical concepts and complex dynamics of the energy markets, my brain somehow created a *bridge of competence* between the Internet revolution and the energy revolution. The framework of the *Flattening of the Energy World* applied the lessons learnt from the "post-mortem," backward-looking, analysis of the Internet revolution to a "pre-mortem," forward-looking analysis, of the energy revolution that was happening in front of our very eyes.

The framework helped us coin new concepts, such as the "Energy Broadband," which explained the complex dynamics of the supercycle in Liquified Natural Gas (meaningless to most people) with the wiring of the oceans with "Internet Broadband" (familiar to most people).

In addition to the interdisciplinary bridges of competence, *The Energy World is Flat* used also historical lessons, or time analogies, such as OPEC's dilemma in the 1980s, which was applied to the then prevailing circumstances in the chapter called "The Btu that broke OPEC's back."

Reflexive Competence

A fascinating feature of the bridges of competence is that they are *reflexive*. The bridges work in both directions. It was fascinating to see how, once the bridges were built, the analogies prompted us—and many people familiar with the Internet revolution—to ask follow-up questions such as "so if the LNG network is the Internet broadband, the Producers are the Telecoms, right?," which continued to "the Telecoms suffered enormous losses via asset write-offs during the bust, I guess that overcapacity in LNG will lead to write-offs for the producers, which will hurt their share price, right?" Bingo!

CHAPTER 3

Gold's Perfect Storm

I first presented the "Lehman Squared" and "Gold's Perfect Storm" investment thesis in a large public forum during the LBMA conference in October 2014.

"Lehman Squared, sounds ominous," tweeted one of the listeners as I spoke.

During the discussion I was asked for my gold price outlook: "a few hundred dollars of downside, and a few thousand dollars of upside," I replied. A view diametrically opposed to the overwhelming pessimistic outlook held by the majority of the market at that time.

"The timing is unsure, it could take 3 to 5 years, who knows, but in my view *much* higher gold prices are just a matter of when, not a matter of if" I added. "But be careful what you wish for!, as much higher gold prices may be the result of some major problem somewhere." The audience grinned.

Barely two months later, on December 15, 2014, the U.S. Federal Reserve hiked rates for the first time since 2006. A highly anticipated move, but exposed some of the excesses that had been built in the system throughout the previous years, which was followed by a major rout in volatility and global equity markets as China's Central Bank, somewhat naively, surprised the market with a 3 percent devaluation of the Chinese Renminbi versus the USD. A move that opened the possibility for further devaluation, forced the Central Bank to intervene aggressively in order to contain the situation. The first real test that the almighty PBOC had to endure. Watch out, because it will not be the last.

The January 2015 "mini-devaluation" was the most clear indication of the "hidden" dangers of currency wars between China, the United States, Europe, and Japan. The compromise reached at the G10 meetings in Shanghai shortly after worked extremely well. If the CNY cannot be devalued without a crisis, then we must appreciate the EUR and JPY (a move that I would describe as "if Mohammed does not go to the mountain, the mountain will go to Mohammed").

The "truce in currency wars" managed to contain the immediate dangers, but I think it is premature to assume that currency wars are over. In my view they are very much alive and will come back alongside protectionist measures.

In any case, this important victory for the Central Banks reinforced the—in my view over complacent—belief that "Central Banks are infallible," which unfortunately incentivizes the wrong behavior and strategies, such as "they will come and rescue us."

More recently, the U.S. Fed has made aggressive moves to normalize monetary policy, while the populist and protectionist wins of Brexit create significant challenges for the United Kingdom and Europe, while Donald Trump's victory in the United States opens the gates for fiscal expansions and a wave of protectionism that creates additional challenges and uncertainty to global markets.

The investment theses presented in this book are very much alive and kicking, if not reinforced by recent developments.

CHAPTER 4

Testing the Limits of Monetary Policy

From Risk-Free Interest to Interest-Free Risk

Gold-Backed Currencies

In 1694, the Bank of England ("BOE") was created and given the responsibility to print notes and back them with gold, becoming the first effort toward independent monetary policy. The BOE was designed to maintain the nation's peg to the gold standard and to trade in a narrow band with other gold-backed currencies.

Over time, other central banks were created and expanded their responsibilities to become the *lender of last resort* to banks during liquidity crises. The metallic currency system evolved to incorporate paper money as a convenient form of legal tender, but always within the bounds of the gold standard, which provided a physical anchor and prevented dilution via printing.

Ben Bernanke, in his book "Great Depression" argues that the world depression was partially caused by a "structurally flawed and poorly managed international gold standard." In his view, what was initially a mild deflationary process began to snowball when the banking and currency crises of 1931 instigated an international "scramble for gold." Sterilization of gold inflows by surplus countries (the United States and France), substitution of gold for FX reserves, and runs on commercial banks all led to increases in the gold backing of money, and consequently to sharp unintended declines in national money supplies.

In Ben Bernanke's opinion, effective international cooperation could have permitted a worldwide monetary expansion despite gold standard constraints, but disputes over World War I reparations and war debts, and the insularity and inexperience of the Federal Reserve, among other factors, prevented the monetary expansion to happen. As a result, individual countries could only escape the deflationary vortex by unilaterally abandoning the gold standard and re-establishing domestic monetary stability.

In 1933, the United States decided to go off the gold standard. Anyone holding significant amounts of gold was mandated to exchange it for the existing fixed price of U.S. dollars. Gold was no longer considered legal tender, and the U.S. Federal Reserve would no longer redeem gold on demand. The dollar was allowed to float freely on FX markets with no guaranteed price in gold.

In 1934, the United States Gold Reserve Act required that all gold held by the Federal Reserve be surrendered and vested in the sole title of the U.S. Treasury and outlawed most private possession of gold, forcing individuals to sell it to the Treasury, who stored it in Fort Knox and other locations.

During the following years, the lack of cooperation among countries within what was an increasingly global and complex financial system led to competitive devaluation of currencies and imbalances, which had been compounded by the World Wars.

In 1944, at Bretton Woods, as a result of the collective conventional wisdom, representatives from all the leading allied nations collectively favored a regulated system of fixed exchange rates, indirectly disciplined by a U.S. dollar tied to gold—a system that relied on a regulated market economy with tight controls on the values of currencies. Flows of speculative international finance were curtailed by shunting them through and limiting them via central banks. This meant that international flows of investment went into foreign direct investment (such as construction of factories overseas) rather than international currency manipulation or bond markets. Although the national experts disagreed to some degree on the specific implementation of this system, all agreed on the need for tight controls.

In 1971, President Richard Nixon unilaterally put an end to the direct convertibility of the U.S. dollar to gold, ending the Bretton Woods system of international financial exchange. A negative balance of payments, growing public debt incurred by the Vietnam War and Great Society programs, and monetary inflation by the Federal Reserve caused the dollar to become increasingly overvalued. The drain on U.S. gold reserves cul-minated with the London Gold Pool collapse in March 1968, and by 1970, the United States had seen its gold coverage deteriorate from 55 to 22 percent. This, in the view of neoclassical economists, represented the point where holders of the dollar had lost faith in the ability of the United States to cut budget and trade deficits.

President Nixon's decision was taken without consulting members of the international monetary system or even his own State Department, and was soon dubbed the *Nixon Shock*.

From Conventional to Unconventional to No Limits

During *normal* times the central bank can manage liquidity requirements and pursue its primary objective of price stability by steering the level of the key interest rates, known as conventional monetary policy.

On the other hand, during *abnormal times*, Central Banks have addi-tional policy measures at their disposal, which include bringing short-term interest rates to zero, introducing guidance of medium to long-term interest rate expectations, expanding the size and changing the compo-sition of the central bank's balance sheet, introducing negative interest rates, and even giving money away via the so-called "helicopter money," all of which are designed to help improve financing conditions and to enhance a credit transmission process that may be significantly impaired.

As discussed in the Lehman Squared investment thesis section, the *acronyms* are mechanisms that "lend a lot of money, to the wrong people, in the wrong size, and at the wrong price."

Quantitative Easing

The first one of the acronyms, QE, defines the process whereby Central Banks expand their balance sheets by buying longer-term government bonds from banks.

QE has a dual objective of bringing down long-term yields in cor-porate bonds and stimulating longer-term investments and aggregate demand, both of which support the objective of price stability.

The effectiveness of QE depends on the ability and willingness of banks to pass on the additional liquidity to the nonfinancial sector.

In addition, QE programs run the risk of accumulating significant losses for the Central Bank, creating concerns about the balance sheet and financial independence, which seriously impede monetary policy. In Europe, these policies need to be mindful of the Treaty requirements relating to the prohibition of *monetary financing*.

The U.S. Federal Reserve gained significant *first mover* advantage adopting QE after Lehman 1.0. Europe and Japan were slow to react and would pay the consequences via much stronger EUR and JPY versus the USD and the CNY. The European crisis that followed a few years later was not a coincidence. Mario Draghi was late to react, but he did it with enormous determination.

The Left Pocket Lends to the Right Pocket

Unconventional monetary policy has enabled the Central Bank (the left pocket) to print and lend money to the Government (the right pocket), a process that questions key basic principles of fiat currencies: Central Bank independence and the risk of Monetary Financing.

> *The epicentre of the problem are the Central Banks, where investors and savers around the world are incentivized—if not forced—to increase the duration in their portfolios, increasing risk of capital losses, liquidity, volatility and correlation beyond what they may be intending or be able to tolerate.*
> —Gold's Perfect Storm, *Financial Times*, Insight Column

Quis custodiet ipsos custodes? Who polices the police, I wonder. A dynamic I discuss in detail in the Lehman Squared section.

Qualitative Easing

Another acronym, "QQE" refers to the Quantitative and Qualitative Easing, which includes "interest rate guidance." The Federal Reserve introduced "the dots," an ingenious communication process that indicated the expectations for forward interest rates by key Fed officials, an effective way to try to bring down and flatten the long-end of the yield curve.

Indirect Quantitative/Credit Easing

The list of acronyms continues with "LTRO," Long-Term Repurchase Obligations. A policy designed to increase the size of the balance sheet by lending to banks at longer maturities against collateral, which includes assets whose markets are temporarily impaired.

The LTRO program was a stroke of genius by the European Central Bank, which achieved a triple objective:

First, provide much needed funding to European Government bonds, some of which on the brink of collapse at the time.

Central Banks have been working overtime to buy time. They have engaged in a series of unprecedented policy initiatives, using experimental measures, and taking enormous risks.
—Mohamed El-Erian

Second, provide much needed help to the European Banks, who had access to liquidity and a risk-free arbitrage whereby they could buy government bonds financed by cheap debt, and capture a healthy spread.

Third, squeeze all the speculative shorts that had been betting against the European Government bonds and the Euro.

Mario Draghi's legend continued to grow.

Negative Interest Rates

The introduction of negative interest rates was a game changer that broke the theoretical ceiling imposed by the Zero Interest Rate Policy ("ZIRP").

Monetary developments in the euro area show no signs of cash substitution, indicating that we are still far away from the "physical lower bound." Central bankers should however be mindful of a potential "economic lower bound," at which the detrimental effects of low rates on the banking sector outweigh their benefits, and further rate cuts risk reversing the expansionary monetary policy stance.
—Benoît Cœuré, Member Executive Committee,
European Central Bank

Negative interest rates have changed the rules of asset valuation, breaking the theoretical ceiling in prices (a zero coupon bond can now trade above par), squeezing-out shorts, squeezing-in underweight positions, effectively perpetuating the bubble in fixed income.

Tax on Cash

Another interpretation of negative interest rates is some form of tax on cash. Clearly, it is very challenging for Central Banks to impose such tax on notes and coins. It is however much easier to apply on bank account balances, on digital money.

> *By permanently printing money, monetary policy credibility heads down the most slippery of slopes. A better solution is to find ways to charge people to hold cash, thereby encouraging spending.*
> —Andy Haldane, Chief Economist, Bank of England

Digital Money

The convenience of digital money (with credit cards, PayPal, Apple Pay, etc.) is reducing the need and appeal of paying with cash. An unstoppable trend that puts policies that tax cash, such as negative interest rates, on a silver tray for Central Banks.

> *A ban on cash would allow negative interest rates to be levied on currency easily and speedily.*
> —Andy Haldane, Chief Economist, Bank of England

Prohibition of Cash

In my view it is just a matter of time before cash disappears. The rationale is clear: avoid tax evasion and illegal activities. The process has already started with the elimination of high denomination notes and introducing legal limits on cash payments.

Virtual Money

Technological developments go further and are supporting the development of virtual currencies such as Bitcoin. I recognize the transformational forces that disrupt the payments and banking industry, but I am very skeptical about the role as a "store of value" and "money." As the world looks for alternatives for fiat currencies, my faith is in gold, not in algorithms.

From Cash Is King to Cash Is Trash

The aggressive policies introduced by the main Central Banks dramatically transformed the perception of cash from "cash is king" in the aftermath of Lehman 1.0, to "cash is trash" as the monetary snowball has pushed interest rates into negative territory.

Direct Credit Easing

The less known acronym, HGCB QE, High Grade Corporate Bond Quantitative Easing, a natural expansion of QE, but applied to nongovernment bonds. Following the mixed success of negative interest rates and the currency wars truce that followed the G20 meetings in Shanghai, the European Central Bank decided to expand QE to high-grade corporate credit in an effort to disintermediate banks, directly addressing liquidity shortages and bringing down credit spreads across commercial paper, corporate bonds, and asset-backed securities.

Yet another major win for Mario Draghi.

Yield Curve Control

This acronym has been coined in Japan. YCC, Yield Curve Control, describes the direct targeting of long-term interest rates (in this case the 10-year) in Japanese Government bonds (JGB).

Yet another creative way to expand the control of long-term interest rates. To achieve that, the BOJ quietly and conveniently removed the restrictions on the duration of its balance sheet, which is yet another step in the direction of "QE infinity" that reinforces the belief (in my view misconception) that Central Banks are in full control.

Something will eventually give. In my view, the JPY has the potential to depreciate very substantially over the medium term. A devaluation that would be welcomed by the Japanese Government, but in my view has the potential to become a "be careful what you wish for" situation, which will enhance currency wars and global imbalances.

Helicopter Money

Already happening, although in a small scale, for now. Helicopter money refers to money that is given (not lent) for consumption purposes. For example, student grants, cash for childcare, cash for elderly care. It is an incentive from the government, that is:

> *Helicopter Money is something that one might legitimately consider.*
> —Janet Yellen

In the current environment, there is a risk that helicopter money could be financed by Central Banks forgiving the debt of governments, known as monetary financing. Following QE, Central Banks have extensive amount of government debt in their balance sheets.

Debt forgiveness would be very inflationary, as the assets in the Central Bank balance sheet are written down to zero, diluting the value of the paper currency sitting on the liability side against them.

The Frog in Boiling Water

Central Banks tend to have objectives that combine some form of *price stability* (such as inflation target) and *growth* (such as achieve full employment). The best case scenario is to fulfill potential in the economy, as close to full employment as possible, as close to the inflation targets as possible. A fine balancing act.

The magic inflation target tends to be 2 percent, which I would describe as a "the frog in the boiling water" policy: small enough to be contained and pass unnoticed in the short term, and large enough to compound very quickly and erode government debt liabilities in the long term.

A compound inflation rate of 2 percent means $1.02 in one year, $1.219 after 10 years, $1.486 after 20 years (worth noting how the interest on interest compounds as 2 percent linear without compounding would be $1.40), and if we continue would be $2.69 after 50 years, well inside an average lifetime.

The Wealth Effect

In addition to diluting the liabilities, inflation creates the so-called *wealth effect* by which is the change in spending that accompanies a change in perceived wealth.

	Conventional	Unconventional	"No Limits"
Short term	Controlled by Central Bank Money Supply Short-Term Target Rates	Controlled by Central Bank Zero Interest Rate Policy (ZIRP)	Controlled by Central Bank Negative Interest Rates Helicopter Money Prohibit Cash?
Long term	Not Controlled by Central Bank Credit Risk Government Inflation expectations	Controlled by Central Bank Government Bond Quantitative Easing (QE), Long Term Repurchase Obligation (LTRO) Qualitative Easing (dots, QQE)	Controlled by Central Bank Yield Curve Control (YCC) Corporate Bond "QE" Public Equity Purchases by Central Bank

The Law of Diminishing Returns

The U.S. Federal Reserve enjoyed a first-mover advantage with the first round of QE, known as "QE1." Encouraged by the success of the program, the perceived fragility of the recovery, and a range of deflationary forces, the U.S. Federal Reserve embarked upon subsequent programs.

The success of the second program, known as "QE2," was less obvious. Indeed, in my opinion it was marginal.

The third program, faced with the law of diminishing returns, which implied "greater volumes for smaller returns," was an open-ended one known as "QE Infinity." The determination of Central Banks was once again proven. The motto "never bet against a Central Banker" reinforced. The impact however was somewhat muted.

Central Banks are conducting bond policy experimentation in real time, and for an unusually prolonged period of time.
—*The Only Game in Town*, Mohamed El-Erian

In my opinion QE1 was needed, QE2 was justified, and QE3 was a mistake, as it reinforced the belief in the Central Bank put, incentivizing the wrong behaviors, and forcing other Central Banks, such as the ECB and BOJ, to defend themselves with even more aggressive measures.

Currency Wars

Central Banks have always positioned QE as a *domestic* policy (reduce long-term yields borrowing costs and improve the credit transmission process), but in practice it is also a powerful *foreign* policy measure via the competitive depreciation of the currency.

The actions from the U.S. Federal Reserve had a direct one-for-one impact on currencies that were pegged to it, such as the Chinese Yuan (CNY, also known as Renminbi RMB). As a result, the competitive devaluation of the USD implied a competitive devaluation of the CNY (a currency arguably already too cheap), which increased their competitiveness against Europe and Japan.

> *Exchange rate policy has been an effective weapon against deflation. A striking example from U.S. history is Franklin Roosevelt's 40 percent devaluation of the dollar against gold in 1933–34, enforced by a program of gold purchases and domestic money creation. The devaluation and the rapid increase in money supply it permitted ended the U.S. deflation remarkably quickly.*
>
> —Ben Bernanke, November 2002

Initially, the ECB, led by the then President Jean-Claude Trichet, was the "good kid on the block" and maintained course with conventional monetary policies. The widening of the interest rate differential between the United States and Europe resulted in a steep appreciation of the EUR, which reached highs close to 1.60 in 2009. Too much for Europe, who would pay in the following years and would lead to an aggressive response. Monetary policy is contagious.

The Theory of Monetary Relativity

Central Banks don't act in isolation. Their decisions factor-in many nondomestic factors, such as exchange rates or interest rate differentials.

Among all, the monetary policy of the United States is the single-most important driver of global monetary policy. Everyone else's monetary policy is run relative to the Fed. Monetary policy is a relative game.

> *Monetary Policy is a relative game. If the Fed had kept rates at 2%, the ECB and BOJ would have never gone negative.*
> —Diego Parrilla, CNBC Interview

In fact, I believe the primary reason why Europe and Japan adopted negative interest rates was to create a positive interest rate differential versus the United States. If USD rates had stayed at 2 percent we would have never seen negative interest rates. A direct implication of what I call the "theory of monetary relativity."

The Duration Bubble

Faced with low or negative interest rates and yields for cash and "risk-free" government bonds, savers and investors have been incentivized—if not forced—to take more risk to generate the fixed income they need. A dynamic that has led to a monetary snowball of lending for longer and longer maturities to generate lower and lower yields: a duration bubble.

Savers who had traditionally been lending for one to three years are today lending for ten, twenty, or even further in order to lock in some positive yields, which is building significant duration risk in their portfolios.

Are investors fully aware of how much more incremental risk they are taking? I don't think so.

The lack of awareness may turn into panic as and when interest rates start to move, as they may experience volatility that they don't want, expect, not may be ready for.

We are witnessing the largest bubble in duration in history. At the time of writing, trillions of dollars of government and corporate bonds are trading at negative nominal yields, a new paradigm to the valuation of fixed income that the market seems to have accepted with complacency.

From Risk-Free Interest to Interest-Free Risk

Finance textbooks have traditionally referred to government bond yields as the risk-free interest rate. The idea is that governments will never default on their obligations because, at the end of the day, they can print paper money to repay their obligations. In Ben Bernanke's words:

> *The U.S. government has a technology, called a printing press (or, today, its electronic equivalent), that allows it to produce as many U.S. dollars as it wishes at essentially no cost. By increasing the number of U.S. dollars in circulation, or even by credibly threatening to do so, the U.S. government can also reduce the value of a dollar in terms of goods and services, which is equivalent to raising the prices in dollars of those goods and services. We conclude that, under a paper-money system, a determined government can always generate higher spending and hence positive inflation.*
>
> —Ben Bernanke, November 2002, then a member of the
> Board of Governors of the U.S. Federal Reserve
> (prior to becoming President)

Under the new paradigm of negative yields, government bonds are earning interest on their borrowings. That is, the lender is paying interest to the borrower (the world in reverse, as in a normal world, the borrower should be paying interest to the lender).

As a consequence, we have transitioned from a world of "risk-free interest" to "interest-free risk." An absurdity that in my view will implode sooner or later, but the market is currently accepting with complacency.

The Theory of Inflation Relativity

Inflation is relative. It is not absolute. Inflation depends on many factors, such as the country we live in (Japan is currently fighting deflation while Venezuela is fighting hyperinflation), our base currency (inflation and deflation can be imported or exported via the FX channel), the stage in our lives, and lifestyle (a family with young children and no property has a very different inflation basket and risk to inflation than a retired elderly person who owns his own house), just to name a few examples.

Despite being relative, we however tend to generalize and model inflation via single indicators such as Consumer Price Index ("CPI") or

Produce Price Index ("PPI") that may give the impression that inflation is an absolute and universal, which is not the case. The convenience of having inflation benchmarks give the government's significant power, as they can conveniently adjust composition and weightings of the inflation basket to achieve their own objectives, and explains why many of these indicators conveniently exclude energy prices or housing, despite being major components of our true inflation basket.

Inflation, Deflation, or Stagflation?

The global financial crisis of 2008 and the lessons learnt during the Great Depression and Japan, the U.S. Federal Reserve engaged in monetary expansion without precedents. The threat of the new nemesis, deflation, was considered as serious as the threat from the traditional and better known enemy: inflation.

Faced with the risk of death by "freezing" (deflation), the Central Banks have undertaken unconventional measures that would raise the risk of death by "boiling" (inflation). Following the lead from Ben Bernanke and the U.S. Federal Reserve, most Central Banks within the G10 leading global economies adopted unconventional expansive policies via contagion. The battle against deflation had turned global.

The lead came from Ben Bernanke, who earned his nickname of "helicopter Ben" following a famous speech in November 2002 (prior to his appointment as Chairman of the U.S. Fed) at the National Economists Club in Washington, D.C. where he referred to economist Milton Friedman's famous "helicopter drop" of money as a viable solution for deflation.

There are, however, second-order and third-order effects in the battle against deflation that complicate things further. For example, financial inflation via monetary policy *without limits* can lead to speculation, gross misallocation of capital, overcapacity, and other forms of bubbles, which as/when they burst can be extraordinarily disinflationary, negating any growth and inflationary benefits. A path-dependent process that could lead to a worst-case scenario of persistent high inflation combined with high unemployment, and stagnant demand, known as *stagflation*.

Energy Deflation

The collapse in energy prices and *The Flattening of the Energy World* have been notable deflationary forces (and a convenient excuse) for the European and Japanese Central Banks to join the monetary party started in the United States, and push ahead with their own monetary experiments.

The Flattening of the Energy World investment thesis I presented in my first book continues to be validated by new evidence and data, and in my opinion, despite the efforts by OPEC and Russia ("ROPEC" as I like to call them) will continue to be the unstoppable trend toward more global, abundant, cleaner, and cheaper energy. Energy deflation will continue to be a key driver of monetary policy, global growth, and geopolitical risks for the foreseeable future.

Monetary Radiation: Cause and (Delayed) Effect

Originated in physics, the principle of causation is that every effect has a cause. Sometimes the effect can be observed immediately. Some other times, the effect can only be observed with a time lag, in some cases a very long time lag.

Sun radiation falls in the category of cause and *delayed* effect. We can spend the day happily in the sun, only feeling the effects during the night or many years later in the form of skin cancer.

Nuclear radiation is also another form of cause and *delayed* effect with devastating effects.

Monetary policy has a delayed effect. In a complex and interrelated world, it is not always obvious to see what caused what effects. Looking back, we can "connect the dots," borrowing Steve Jobs' famous lines. But it is possible that we may overexpose ourselves, creating problems later. This is known as "being behind the curve" in monetary policy, which introduces a sense of time and path dependency in monetary policy.

Kicking the Can Down Monetary Road

There is an almost philosophical debate behind monetary policy without limits. It is clear that the actions of the Central Banks helped avoid an even larger crisis in 2008. It is also clear that those same actions may be artificially inflating asset prices, leading to greater inequality. The rich (who own financial assets) get richer, and the poor (who don't own financial assets) get poorer and lose purchasing power.

A generational debate that is leading to growing populism and protectionism, among other second-order and third-order unintended consequences of monetary inflation. More on this later.

The Point of No Return: BOJ JGB OMG

In my opinion, a country such as Japan has passed the point of no return in their monetary policy. As of December 2016, the Bank of Japan (BOJ) owned 41.3 percent of the total JGB market. The BOJ purchased 10 trillion yen during the month of November 2016 alone which annualized implies at a pace of accumulation of over 13 percent per year. Fast forward two years of accumulation at the current pace and years, and the BOJ will own close to 70 percent of the outstanding JGB market. A situation I describe as *BOJ, JGB, OMG* (Bank of Japan, Japanese Government Bonds, Oh My God).

I refer to *The Point of No Return* to a situation when the addiction or dependency has reached such an extreme that the patient can no longer survive without the support. In the case of Japan, an effort to normalize monetary policy by hiking interest rates could lead to significant capital losses in investments and a large rise in debt servicing costs, which could contribute to a larger crisis.

As a result, I no longer believe that the JGB market will ever fail. It is much more likely that the "left pocket" (the Central Bank) will forgive the right pocket (the Government). A process called monetary financing, which would result in a significant devaluation of the Japanese Yen. More on this later.

An issue to consider when implementing nonconventional policies is the risk of hindering the functioning of markets by substituting or interfering with them. Agents' refinancing needs may become excessively dependent on operations settled with the central bank. In other words, financing conditions may become overly attractive as a result of central bank operations and may crowd out other channels, reducing the incentives for restarting normal market conditions.

—Lorenzo Bini Smaghi, Member of the ECB Executive Board

Japan is in my view the most extreme example, but not the only one. In Europe, the situation is still under control, but at the time of writing, negative yields are a reality not only in the government bond market, but also in many short-term corporate debts. A situation that I call "flirting with the point of no return."

The world has largely exhausted the scope for central bank improvisation as a growth strategy.

—Larry Summers

China is in my view another major risk in the global financial system. In my article published at Spanish newspaper *El Mundo* titled "The great devaluation of China," published early 2016, I analyzed the need and rationale for a major devaluation versus the USD. In my view, China is a strong candidate to adopt many of the unconventional monetary policies used in the West as and when required, which will exacerbate the currency wars and add significant deflationary pressures to the rest of the world. As the marginal consumer of many commodities, a 10 percent devaluation of the CNY has the potential to result in a 10 percent sell-off in USD-denominated commodity prices (so that CNY-denominated prices stay constant). Watch this space, because it is the epicenter of many of the global imbalances and possibly the next global crisis.

Emerging markets are in my view "caught between a rock and a hard place." They have been major beneficiaries of the "yield-seeking bubble" as investors seek for income-generating alternatives in other markets. The hot money and speculative flows can be very distorting both on the way in and the way out, as we well know.

Central Bank Leadership Risk

The surge in duration risk has been extraordinary. Many investors have extended the average maturity of their bond portfolio in order to generate some positive yield, incurring a somewhat hidden risk: election risk.

What happens in Europe if Angela Merkel and Mario Draghi were not re-elected? What happens in Japan if Shinzo Abe and Haruhiko Kuroda were not re-elected? What if the newcomers were to unwind their policies? As described in the *Point of No Return*, perhaps the newcomers have no choice but to continue the current direction. We will find out in the not-too-distant future.

The Myth of Central Banks' Infallibility

I have referred several times to the so-called "Central Bank Put," the complacent belief (in my view misconception) that Central Banks are in full control and will continue to be in control no-matter-what.

The perception that Central Banks will keep interest rates low for the foreseeable future creates a very powerful, almost unstoppable, *monetary snowball* effect. The successes of the Central Bank feed on themselves and strengthen the perception of infallibility. More on this later.

Exit Strategy

Exit Plan A for Central Banks is to smoothly normalize monetary policy when the economy rebounds and inflationary prospects are back in line with the Central Bank's price stability objective.

The normalization requires some careful planning and execution. First, devising the right *sequence* for the phasing out of the conventional and unconventional monetary policy accommodation. Second, deciding on the *speed* at which the unconventional accommodation is removed. A careful balance, as withdrawing liquidity in such large quantities too quickly would trigger a substantial contractionary monetary policy shock whereby policymakers risk choking off the economic recovery or imposing heavy capital losses on lenders. On the other hand, keeping such exceptional measures in place for too long might aggravate the upside risks to price stability and plant the seeds for future imbalances in financial markets. Getting the timing right in withdrawing additional liquidity is likely to be decisive in order to ensure a noninflationary recovery. Generally speaking, the lower the reversibility of the nonconventional operations, the larger the risk of being *behind the curve* when the macroeconomic and financial market situation improves.

The speed of unwinding of unconventional measures would depend on their degree of reversibility. Some of the unwinding would happen automatically as central bank programmes become increasingly unattractive as financial conditions normalise. As a result, the central bank's balance sheet would decline automatically as demand for its funds decreases.

—Lorenzo Bini Smaghi, Member of the ECB Executive Board

Ceteris paribus, the unwind of unconventional policies by Central Banks implies the liquidation of massive holdings of government bonds and other assets, which investors and savers would need to buy in order to keep the level of government debt constant. Effectively a reversal of the past few years, which in my view could expose the duration bubble and other forms of financial inflation that have been built in the system.

Alternatively, the Government could buy-back its outstanding debt prior to the maturity. Wishful thinking in my view.

Exit Plan B for Central Banks is to maintain by current stimuli by holding the government bonds to expiry. At that point in time, the Government may decide whether to repay or refinance the debt. Plan B is identical to Plan A, except that it gives the Central Bank and the Government plenty of time. The challenges remain the same though.

Exit Plan C for Central Banks is to forgive the debt to the Governments. A process that goes against the principle of independence of Central Banks and, as discussed earlier in the section "BOJ JGB OMG," could lead to monetary financing as the "left pocket" (the Central Bank) forgives the debt of the right pocket (the Government). As a believer of the Austrian School of Economics, or "no free-lunch economics" as I call it, something would give and in my view the imbalances would manifest via a significant devaluation of the currency, which would revive and exacerbate currency wars. A monetary supercycle in the making. More on this shortly.

CHAPTER 5

Testing the Limits of Credit Markets

The Complacent and Desperate Search for Yield

Faced with low or negative interest rates and yields in "risk-free" government bonds, savers and investors have been incentivized—or rather, forced—to take more duration risk to generate the fixed income required to meet their liabilities. A self-enforced process of lending for longer and longer maturities in exchange of lower and lower yields that in my view is leading to the largest duration bubble in history.

The exact same dynamics are incentivizing—or rather forcing—investors and savers to take more credit risk, lending to weaker and weaker credits for lower and lower yields, inflating a bubble in the credit and equity markets.

The Credit Spread Steamroller

The price action and lower financing costs have had a positive impact on fundamentals, a clear application of George Soros' reflexivity theory, which argues that "fundamentals impact prices, but prices also drive fundamentals." A virtuous cycle of price appreciation and ever-improved fundamentals. More on this later.

The virtuous cycle of lower borrowing costs and better fundamentals behaves like a steamroller that crushes credit risk premiums and benefits the weakest players the most. Look at my country, Spain. What's fundamentally changed since 2012 when the 10-year bond reached a yield of 7.5 percent, and was on the brink of collapse? Fundamentals have not changed that much, and in my view do not justify the swing from one extreme to the other. The basic and simple explanation is we avoided a disaster (thanks Mario!) but the reversal toward current levels and negative yields is equally excessive and can only be justified by the Central Bank buying without limits.

High yield credit markets and emerging markets are clear examples of markets that have seen record levels of issuance, as yet another example of demand from investors looking for yield creates supply from borrowers looking to take advantage of the ultra-low rates.

Fiscal Expansion: The Prudent Imprudence

Demand creates supply. It is true for commodity markets, and true for credit markets.

The initial rounds of QE consisted of Central Bank buying the existing inventory of government bonds from investment banks and institutional clients, hoping they would put the money to work. A form of indirect credit easing, as discussed.

In the case of Japan and Europe, the size of the QE programs is so large that the Central Bank is either monopolizing the demand and/or literally running out of inventory to buy. That's how imbalanced the market is.

To my surprise, Larry Summers, one of the most respected economists in the world, wrote an article in the *Financial Times* called "the prudent imprudence" where he argued for the merits of fiscal expansion. An analysis that in my view completely misses the point and encourages a "triple-up" in risk (monetary policy without limits was a "double up" in my view).

> *Bond market tells us there is not enough debt.*
> *Like homeowners, governments can borrow more when rates are low.*
> *Maastricht 60% debt to GDP target was designed at 5% rates.*
> *We can borrow more.*
>
> —Larry Summers

A dynamic that reminds me of someone stepping into the bank and asking "how much can I borrow?" instead of asking "what can I afford?" The fact that someone is willing to lend me cheap money does not imply

I should borrow it. Financing should be a function of the investment opportunities available. Unfortunately, many countries have a mixed track record putting the money to work. Indeed, fiscal expansions tend to be very short-termist measures designed to win votes and not necessarily long-term growth.

> *Ironically, fiscal expansion, historically considered imprudent, is now the only prudent way forward.*
>
> —Larry Summers

Credit, as any other form of insurance, just because interest rates are at a negative, doesn't mean life expectancy or car accidents are going to change in terms of an actuarial basis.

Trump coming into office opens a whole new chapter in terms of, once again, pushing the limits of credit markets: "Let's borrow more! Let's build more!" In my view, the United States has the stronger case for fiscal expansion and infrastructure spending. The other extreme is possibly China, where the tool has been used and abused to a very large extent.

Structural Reform and Restructuring

The two easy solutions: #1 print more money, and #2 borrow more, prevent governments from tackling the necessary structural reform and restructure.

A good example is China, who despite having clear plans to tackle imbalances, was forced to step back and do "more of the same" (intervene and provide monetary and fiscal stimuli) in order to try to contain the situation. This dynamic also contributes to delay or avoid hard decisions, supporting *zombie companies* that only survive on subsidies. A short-term patch that make the problem bigger, not smaller.

The Gross Misallocation of Capital

The record level of issuance in the private and public markets translates broadly into a combination of more liquidity (money not at work), more working capital (money at work short term), and more fixed investments (money at work long term).

We know from history that there are three possible outcomes when we put the money to work: Some money will finance valuable projects (NPV > 0). Some money will finance marginal projects (Net Present Value, NPV = 0). And some money will finance bad projects, overcapacity, and speculation (NPV < 0). It is impossible to know with certainty how much money may have been grossly misallocated. Only time will tell.

During the Lehman 1.0 crisis the lending from the acronyms found its way primarily to real estate and infrastructure in the developed world. This time around, the lending from the new acronyms is finding its way to virtually everywhere. A big concern.

Inflating the Capital Structure

The virtuous cycle has a direct impact across the entire capital structure. As a result, there is yet another parallel bubble across equity markets that is benefiting from the exact same dynamics as duration and credit.

Furthermore, Central Banks' buying spree has not been limited to government bonds. As discussed in the previous chapter, Central Banks have also been buying high-grade credit and even equities. A massive reinforcement of the perception of Central Bank infallibility, as in principle they can print infinite amounts of their own paper to buy anything. Back to the "no free-lunch economics," I believe this dynamic is unsustainable and will lead to major inflation and currency devaluations.

Second-Order Effects

Inequality, widening the gap between rich and poor, is in my view one of the unintended consequences of monetary policy without limits and globalization. The statistics speak for themselves, with 1 percent of the world's population holding over 50 percent of the wealth.

Further, neo-protectionism in the United Kingdom (Brexit) and the United States (Trump) have emerged as a response to immigration and globalization. A new dimension and source of uncertainty to the global markets.

In addition, political fragmentation and political paralysis are also emerging as obstacles to some of the structural reforms that Central

Banks are asking and hoping for. Both extreme right and extreme left are gaining support across Europe.

Taxation

Fiscal expansion provides a short-term boost to the economy by bringing future consumption forward at the expense of lower growth and higher taxation down the line. A bet designed with the hope that the path dependency will be NPV positive, but more often than not these measures are designed with electoral objectives rather than economic ones.

The Shadow Banking System

There are other more structural factors that are also contributing to a credit bubble. The most dangerous in my view is the shadow banking in China. A process that has emerged from constraints and inefficiencies in the Chinese credit transmission process.

There is extensive literature on this issue, which describes the dangers of the many forms of shadow banking, including off-balance sheet lending via structured products. Explosive leveraged instruments that take enormous carry and credit bets: a time bomb in my view.

The Epicenter

The bubble in duration across the government bond market is the Epicenter of all the other bubbles, but in my view will not be the catalyst of a potential crisis.

For example, I used to believe that the bubble in the JGB market was unsustainable and would eventually blow up. My current view is that the JGB market will remain inflated for the foreseeable future, but something else will give in. As a believer in "no free-lunch economics," I believe the imbalances will show somewhere else, and in the case of Japan, and other countries following its path, it will happen via the FX channel with major devaluations down the road.

As discussed, I believe that Japan has passed the point of no return and JGBs are already "too big to fall." The pillar of Central Bank independence has been compromised, and in my view the Japanese Government will rely on the printing press to finance, refinance, and eventually repay their debt via monetary financing and "debt forgiveness," a highly inflationary scenario that will weaken the yen to levels we have not seen in living memory. A "be careful what you wish for" type of scenario. But time will tell.

The Catalysts

There are many catalysts that could expose the imbalances in the system.

First, related to testing the limits of monetary policy. The catalysts would expose the bubble in duration, which could be triggered by a change in Central Bank leadership and policies.

Second, related to testing the limits of credit markets. The catalysts would expose any of the parallel bubbles across high yield credit, emerging markets, or equities among many candidates. These will fall by their own weight.

Third, related to testing the limits of fiat currencies, as per the example from Japan discussed earlier. The catalysts would likely arise from currency wars and competitive devaluations.

All these represent some of the known unknowns, to which we would need to add geopolitical risks and other unknown unknowns.

Stressing the Stress Tests

In my view, stress tests on investment banks played a key role in the Lehman 1.0 crisis. Until then, the true magnitude of the problem was unknown. The uncertainty created a vicious cycle of distrust that shut down all lending between banks, creating an implosion at the core of the markets, which spread out very quickly to other sectors.

The stress tests told us how big the problem was. They told us how much recapitalization the banks needed. They set the beginning of the end of the crisis, as monetary policy and government intervention brought back some confidence into the system.

Of course, it took a long time to get all the "domino pieces" back in place. But the determination from the Central Banks and the Governments to do "whatever it takes" was founded on some more tangible estimates in the form of stress tests.

This time around it may be different. The shadow banking system is by definition unregulated. Its true size is not known. Many investors take comfort on the large reserves of the Chinese Central Bank, ignoring the fact that many of those assets are subject to netting and may account to a fraction of the problem. A very scary situation that the Chinese Government will fight at all cost.

Return *on* Capital versus Return *of* the Capital

The desperate search for yield ignores or downplays the risk of capital losses. As and when the yield-seeking bubble bursts, investors will once again focus on the return of their capital instead of the return on their capital, an extremely bullish scenario for gold, volatility, and selective real assets.

Time will tell if Central Banks and Governments will be able to engineer a smooth solution to the challenges ahead, or if the remedy will be worse than the disease. Monetary policy without limits will lead to very wild and bumpy ride and a larger crisis than the one we have been trying to resolve: a perfect storm for gold.

CHAPTER 6

Testing the Limits of Fiat Currencies

No Free-Lunch Economics

I am a believer in the "no free-lunch" Austrian school of economics. I believe that monetary policy and credit markets have limits and that the current path is unsustainable and something has to give.

Fiat Currencies

As Voltaire warned us: "The value of paper money eventually converges to its intrinsic value: paper," a very skeptical view of the incentives and behavior of the Governments issuing such paper.

Indeed, fiat currencies are an act of *faith* in the Central Bank and Government who created it. History is full of examples of Governments who tried to finance their wars and/or social programs by printing money, taking advantage of the ignorance of their people and/or assuming they had no choice. They were wrong.

The Two Sides of the Monetary Coin

Monetary policy and fiat currencies are two sides of the same coin. If we destroy one side, we will most likely destroy the other. As such, our efforts to test the limits of monetary policy translate directly into testing the limits of fiat currencies. The checkmate of this game and the channel by which Central Banks and Governments are forced to re-establish the trust, or else.

A central bank's balance sheet is the foundation on which both money and monetary policy are built. A central bank's liabilities define the quantity of so-called base money in circulation. And the interest rate

on central bank money defines monetary policy. In that sense, central bank money and monetary policy are two sides of the same coin.
—Andy Haldane, Chief Economist, Bank of England

Needless to say, gold-backed currencies have no monetary policy or seigniorage. The duty of the Central Bank—once upon a time—was to ensure that all paper money was backed by gold. A physical feature that protected the currency from potential dilution via printing.

The decoupling of gold from money has not only opened the gate for Governments to expand and contract the monetary base to achieve its objectives of financial stability, but it has also opened the door to the dangerous slippery slope of seigniorage and monetary financing.

Easy Solution #1: Print More Money

It would be nice if we could *print* our way out of every problem. History is full of examples of economies, such as Argentina, Zimbabwe, or more recently Venezuela, who have tried and failed. Many other developed countries, such as Japan or Europe, are behaving similarly—if not worse—but can get away with it, for now.

I found myself doing extraordinary things that weren't in the textbooks. Then the IMF asked the U.S. to please print money. The whole world is now practicing what they have been saying I should not. I decided that God had been on my side and had come to vindicate me.
—Gideon Gono, Former Governor, Reserve Bank Zimbabwe

Easy Solution #2: Borrow More Money

It would also be nice if we could *borrow* our way out every problem. Here again, many countries such as Russia, Mexico, or Greece have tried and failed. Some developed and developing countries such as Japan or China are behaving similarly—if not worse—doubling and tripling their bets with the invaluable help of their partner in crime, the Central Bank.

Gold's Perfect Storm Investment Thesis

I first presented the *Lehman Squared* and *Gold Perfect Storm* investment thesis during the Annual LBMA Gold Conference in October 2015 that was being held in Vienna. The sentiment across market participants was extraordinarily pessimistic at the time. Gold prices were under immense pressure ahead of the much-anticipated first hike by the U.S. Federal Reserve. My investment thesis and asymmetric outlook were highly contrarian to the depressed and pessimistic consensus and positioning of the market, which only reinforced my view that gold was about to reverse course.

My Gold Perfect Storm thesis reached a global scale a few months later with the publication by the *Financial Times* of my article by the same name which, to my surprise and honor, was published on the front page of the written edition on June 8, 2016. An extract of the article described the investment as follows:

> Gold prices have rallied over 30 percent since the lift-off in U.S. interest rates in December. A sharp reversal in pricing, sentiment, and positioning driven by a myriad of macro and micro factors and has left the gold bears and bulls as polarized as ever.
>
> The bearish camp, which has featured prominent and respected analysts such as Goldman Sachs, tends to have a constructive view on the US dollar, the ability to raise interest rates, normalize global monetary policy, and generally a benign view on the global economy and inflationary risks.
>
> The bullish camp, which I subscribe to, tends to have a more pessimistic view on the global economy and the unintended consequences of monetary policy without limits, and sees the recent price action as the beginning of a multiyear bull-run in gold. My view that there is a perfect storm for gold based on three closely interrelated dynamics, whereby central banks and global markets are both testing the limits of monetary policy and credit markets as well as the boundaries of fiat currencies.
>
> Gold's Perfect Storm investment thesis argues that gold is at the beginning of a multiyear bull market with "a few hundred dollars of downside, and a few thousand dollars of upside." The framework is based on three phases: testing the limits of monetary policy, testing the limits of credit markets, and testing the limits of fiat currencies

Gresham's Law: Good Money and Bad Money

I first came across Gresham's law in Peter Bernholz's book, "Monetary Regimes and Inflation: History, Economic and Political Relationships," a somewhat dry but extraordinary foundation to understand the current dynamics in the global currency markets.

Gresham's law introduces two concepts: good money and bad money, and how they interact through inflationary and hyperinflationary scenarios.

Phase 1: "Bad Money Replaces Good Money"

The concepts can be easily understood via a historical case study. It all starts with a monetary system backed by physical gold. There is paper money, but it is backed on a one-by-one basis by gold. Let's assume, for the sake of argument, that there were 1 million currency units backed by 1 million gold units.

The Government enters into war and decides to finance its war (pay the soldiers, etc.) by printing paper. Initially, everyone assumes that the paper money is backed by gold. Nobody knows that paper is being printed. There is more paper money in circulation, but inflation is contained. Trade continues normally, but somehow paper transactions start to dominate. A few smart people prefer to pay in paper and accumulate gold, and as a result *bad money* (paper) starts to replace *good money* (gold) from transactions.

Phase 2: "Good Money Replaces Good Money"

At some point, inflation starts becoming more obvious to the public. The butcher, the baker, the smith, can feel that there seems to be more paper and goods. Trade starts to demand payment in gold instead of paper, which accelerates inflation. The soldiers and providers of the Government, aware of inflationary pressures, demand higher wages and prices, which leads to the government to accelerate the speed of money printing. The gradual loss of confidence in paper money gives way to a phase where good money (gold) replaces bad money (paper), which accelerates inflation further. At one point, inflation explodes and gets out of control.

Far from giving up easily, there are examples in history when the Government introduced death penalty for not accepting paper currencies. A good reminder to those wondering how far governments could go with their monetary policy without limits.

Eventually, and ironically, the Government demands payment of taxes in kind (corn, meat, timber, etc.) and stops accepting their own paper money. The last nail in the coffin for the paper currency.

The Government is then forced to stop the printing in an effort to re-establish the trust in their creation, their paper money. After a period of extreme volatility, the value of paper money is anchored to gold. The fair value is a function of how much money was printed. If the Government printed 9 million incremental paper units, then the new value of gold will be 10 times higher than prior to the currency crisis. I call this a monetary supercycle.

Seigniorage

Central Banks discovered very quickly the benefits of seigniorage, which is the difference between the value of money and the cost to produce it.

> *Seigniorage is the difference between the value of money and the cost to produce it.*
>
> —www.investopedia.com

In the early days of money this was done by casting coins with denominations that were greater than the value of gold required to produce it.

Today, what is the cost of issuing *paper money*, say a $100 note? Not much.

And the cost of issuing *digital money*, say a $100 book entry? Even less.

The difference is a windfall for the Government. Thank you very much. And why it is just a matter of time before they get their hands via taxation or outright prohibition of other forms of virtual money outside of Government control, such as crypto currencies.

The Monetary Supercycle

Gresham's law provides a clear framework of "no free-lunch economics." The gold price must appreciate to reflect the exact amount of paper money that has been printed.

Supercyclical behavior is the norm in commodity markets. I have gone through several of them during my career and that is why the concept is very obvious and intuitive to me. At the core, the physical nature of commodities means we can't print crude oil, or copper, or corn, or gold. A supercycle works as follows:

A typical supercycle starts with overcapacity, whereby supply is greater than demand and leads to the accumulation of inventories. This is a period of low commodity prices and poor economic returns, which discourages investment in new productive capacity and encourages demand and consumption. Demand growth starts closing the gap with supply and eventually the market rebalances and goes into a deficit, whereby inventory levels are withdrawn and could eventually run out. Prices start to go up to incentivize investment, substitution, and demand destruction. In the absence of inventories and elastic supply (it takes time to build mines, oil fields, etc.) the only way to adjust the market is by demand destruction, which explains the surge in commodity prices and the backwardation in the forward curves (premium for immediate availability). How high commodity prices spike is largely a function of the price elasticity of demand and substitution. In the case of crude oil, for example, the market was extremely inelastic: in order to destroy 2 percent of demand, oil prices had to go up by 100 percent (double). In the old days, it would take at least 10 years to develop a new oil field, which explains why the supercycles in energy have been so wild. In other markets, such as copper, it takes on average three years to develop a mine. In the case of shipping, the supply response can be less than one year.

Back to gold, we have been accumulating and issuing paper money without any tangible backing, such as gold. The value of money is an act of faith on the Government and Central Banks that created it.

Room of Mirrors

The current global currency system can be compared to a room of mirrors, where the asset and liabilities of the Central Banks balance sheets are mainly paper and government bonds, their own (which they can print) and someone else's (which someone else can print), plus some historical legacy of gold that once-upon-a-time backed the currency.

The relative value of the main global currencies, such as the USD, EUR, or JPY is set by the free trade of their exchange rates in the markets. Some currencies, such as the CNY (Chinese Yuan aka Renminbi) or the SAR (Saudi Arabian Riyal) are pegged to the USD. A move where they give up their monetary policy in exchange for some perceived stability, which, as part of the "no free-lunch" school of economics, leads to imbalances somewhere else, in the form of inflation/deflation, accumulation of reserves, shadow banking, and other complex dynamics. A time bomb in my view.

Monetary Asset that Is No One's Liability

In this context of global cross-holdings of currencies and government debt, gold stands out as the only asset that is no one's liabilities.

Shadow Gold Price for USD

The size of the Central Banks balance sheets has steadily expanded over the past few decades, but has dramatically accelerated with monetary policy without limits, while Central Bank gold reserves have stayed relatively stable.

The application of Gresham's to calculate a theoretical monetary price of gold was coined by Paul Brodsky and Lee Quaintance as *shadow gold price* (SGP), which extrapolates the value of gold from the end of Bretton Woods adjusted by the growth in base money versus growth in U.S. Government actual gold holdings. Assuming a reserve conversion ratio of 100 percent the gold shadow price would be 18,000 USD. And this is just for the USD, which happens to be the largest gold holder in the world.

In 1914, the Federal Reserve Act stipulated a minimum gold cover of 40 percent, which was subsequently reduced to 25 percent between 1945 and 1971, before it was completely removed with the end of Bretton Woods. Under those reserve cover ratio, the price of gold would need to be adjusted on a prorated basis.

Shadow Gold Price in Other Currencies

The SGP for the Japanese Yen is astronomical due to the combination of a high numerator (base money in local currency terms) with a small denominator (gold reserves). Japan is the 8th largest Central Bank in terms of official gold reserves with 765.2 tons, equivalent to less than 25 million ounces of gold, and valued at less than $30b at current market prices. To put in context, the official gold reserves of Japan would buy less than 5 percent of the market cap of Apple.

The SGP and other similar valuation methods are theoretical data points, not meant to be price targets, but make clear the extent of the money printing and the dilution of paper currencies versus gold reserves. A dynamic that is consistent with the view that "gold has a few hundred dollars of downside and a few thousand dollars of upside."

Monetary Asset of Choice

I was once asked in a meeting, and why gold and not bananas? The idea behind the question was: what makes gold so unique? Should all real assets benefit in parallel from inflation and money printing?

It is true that pure *parallel shift* in inflation caused by money printing should inflate all assets more or less proportionally. In that sense, the price of bananas, land, crude oil, or gold, should all go up in tandem.

The monetary supercycle is not a parallel shift. It is a rebasing of the printing of monetary base versus a monetary asset of choice, which in my view is likely to be gold for a number of reasons, including its unique physical and chemical properties that make it the store or value of choice by many civilizations for over 3,000 years, and its scarcity, which prevent it from excessive dilution via mine production.

In the 17th century, Sweden introduced a copper-based monetary system that worked very well until the world copper price slumped following the discoveries of large mines in Africa and the Americas. Sweden's *daler* had a much greater face value than the copper content market value and was easy to counterfeit, which resulted in the rapid loss of the seniority premium, wiping out the purchase power and savings of many people of Sweden.

Paper currencies eventually converge to their fair value: paper.

—Voltaire

In addition to its physical and chemical properties and its rarity, gold counts with the support of many influential governments. China and Russia, for example, have been steadily accumulating gold reserves over the past few years as part of a parallel battle for the reserve currency status.

The Battle for World's Reserve Currency

The United States and the U.S. dollar have been enjoying the privileges of being the World's Reserve Currency since the 1930s, when it took over from the Sterling Pound.

As the Reserve Currency of the World, the USD is held as the dominant share of foreign exchange reserves, serves as the base for international transactions, and is often considered a hard currency with safe-haven status, which has allowed the U.S. Government to finance itself with foreign capital in large quantities and more cheaply.

The U.S. Government is currently the largest holder of gold with 8,133 tons, with current market value circa $300 billion, which equates to less than 50 percent of Apple's Market Cap. Not as large as one might have thought.

The Chinese Government has been a steady buyer of gold over the past few years, and has supported the trade and ownership of gold by its citizens with the development of the Shanghai Gold Exchange (SGE), which has already surpassed the almighty New York Mercantile Exchange (NYMEX) and London interbank market in terms of daily volumes. As of writing, the official Chinese gold reserves stand at 1,838 tons, approximately $70 billion, and 2 percent FX Reserves.

Central Banks will most likely continue to be net buyers of gold, led by China, Russia, and India, which will likely lead to the steady flow of gold from West to East.

The Monetary Supercycle

The Gold Perfect Storm investment thesis argues that testing the limits of monetary and credit markets will eventually also test the limits of fiat currencies. The loss of faith in paper and digital money could force the governments to anchor the value of their devalued currencies to a credible base.

The USD and gold are the best candidates to play the role of *good money*, but that the "USD emperor has no clothes either" and gold will eventually prevail as the monetary asset of choice. A monetary supercycle that will result in a very significant appreciation of gold against most currencies, but particularly against those that are "bad money disguised as good money," as it is the case for the Japanese Yen, and possibly the Chinese Yuan.

CHAPTER 7

A Premortem Analysis

Soros Reflexivity

How can we justify the behavior of Central Banks and Governments, testing the limits of monetary policy and credit markets? The answer in my view is given by Soros Reflexivity theory, which states that "fundamentals drive prices, but prices also drive fundamentals."

The European Government bond crisis was a good example of how Soros' Reflexivity theory works. During the early stages, the crisis in small economies such as Greece was not impacting larger economies such as Italy or Spain. "We are ok," would say their respective finance ministers. As the crisis advanced, a domino effect of forced liquidations and contagion pushed the borrowing costs of Italy and Spain higher. "We are ok. We don't need any help" would argue the finance ministers, but the doubts were growing among the investors. A vicious cycle of liquidation, higher borrowing costs, more liquidation, which eventually sent the yield of the Spanish 10-year bond close to 7.5 percent p.a., a level considered to be a *tipping point* where the costs of servicing the debt dominate government finances. The "we need help" from the investors would be followed by "I knew it" from the investors. The ironic thing is that the Government was genuinely "ok," but the price action and higher borrowing costs had tilted them to "not being ok."

The opposite dynamic, a virtuous cycle is also true. A dynamic that Central Banks understand very well and have applied with monetary policy without limits. The Central Banks know they can control interest rates and inflate prices in government bonds as much as they want, which they know will translate into higher prices across other asset prices. Their hope is that prices pull fundamentals higher via the wealth effect, increased investment, increased consumption, and ultimately real growth. Or at least that's their plan.

From New Normal to T-Junction

The global financial crisis of 2008 gave way to a regime known as *new normal*, which has been characterized by low growth, rising inequality, political dysfunction, and in some cases social tensions. The concept of *new normal* is attributed to Mohamed El-Erian, and later evolved to the *new mediocre* coined by Christine Lagarde, IMF Director.

> *The good news is that the recovery continues; we have growth; we are not in a crisis. The not-so-good news is that the recovery remains too slow, too fragile, and risks to its durability are increasing. Certainly, we have made much progress since the great financial crisis. But because growth has been too low for too long, too many people are simply not feeling it. This persistent low growth can be self-reinforcing through negative effects on potential output that can be hard to reverse. The risk of becoming trapped in what I have called a "new mediocre" has increased.*
>
> —Christine Lagarde, IMF Director

In his latest book titled "The Only Game in Town," Mohamed El-Erian moves away from the new normal and introduces a new dynamic he refers to as "T-junction."

> *The new normal is getting increasingly exhausted. For those who care to look, signs of stress are multiplying—so much that the path of the global economy is likely to end up soon, and potentially quite suddenly. The current road, engineered and maintained by hyperactive central banks will likely end within the next three years, if not earlier, to be replaced with a T-junction that leads to one of two roads that fundamentally contrast in their implications.*
>
> —*The Only Game in Town*, Mohamed El-Erian

The "T-junction" describes a binary outcome: we will either go left or right, but will not remain in the middle of the road boring low growth. A sober warning to those thinking the current path is sustainable.

Diplomatic Neutrality

At the time of writing, Mohamed El-Erian assigned a balanced "50/50" probability to the positive and negative outcomes. The symmetric probability gives the impression that the risks are balanced, but ignores the stark asymmetry of outcomes, and that's why I call it "diplomatic neutrality." Let me explain in more detail.

Symmetry of Probability

El-Erian assigns a 50 percent probability of positive and negative outcome. Optically balanced. So far so good.

Asymmetry of Outcome

El-Erian understands that the outcomes are highly asymmetric and imbalanced.

The positive scenario has limited upside. To keep things simple, we can assume that fundamentals converge toward the inflated prices. If this scenario materializes, the upside in the markets is limited as the good news is already priced in.

The negative scenario has much greater downside. To keep things simple, we can assume that prices converge to the fundamentals. If this scenario materializes, the downside in the markets is much greater as the good news is already priced in.

The ECB is mindful of these risks. In the euro area, the potential adverse impact on bank profitability, if it materialises, would be compounded by low growth prospects and a legacy of high non-performing loans. The current conditions of financial intermediation suggest, however, that the economic lower bound is safely below the current level of the deposit facility rate and that the impact of negative rates, combined with the APP and forward guidance, has clearly been net positive.

—Benoît Cœuré, Member Executive, Committee European
Central Bank

Negative Expectancy

The combination of symmetric probabilities and asymmetric outcomes is negative expectancy. Let's use a very simple example, where we have a 50/50 chance of making $1 or losing $10. Clearly not a very attractive bet.

A Premortem Analysis

Premortem is a method that uses *prospective hindsight* (imagining that an event has already occurred), which can help us bring down mental barriers and identify risks that were ignored due to biases.

The Virtuous Cycle ("Hoping for the Better")

The idea of the premortem is to assume that the positive outcome has already happened. The Lehman Squared and Gold Perfect Storm investment theses proved out to be wrong. Let's walk our way back and understand how we "did it."

A happy premortem starts with the normalization of U.S. monetary policy that leads to a stronger USD, which allows the European and Japanese Central Bank to normalize their respective monetary policies and remain competitive. The monetary incentives provided to the governments are used for productive projects that generate sustainable employment and support economic activity, which leads to increased fiscal revenues. Central Banks policies have also helped banks, which are now stronger and able to engage in lending, supporting investments and economic activities. The duration bubble is unwound slowly, with capital losses on investments compensated by solid economic activity and growth. China is able to float the CNY in an orderly fashion. Global demand and domestic consumption in China remains strong, and the Government is able to go ahead with the restructuring and reform plans, which slow down growth but reduce the imbalances and risks of a credit crisis. A happy ending.

The Vicious Cycle ("Preparing for the Worst")

A less-happy premortem starts a reversal of the normalization of U.S. monetary policy as a much stronger USD is viewed as a threat to the U.S. economy. Protectionism creates barriers to global trade and generates inflationary pressures with limited growth. The European and Japanese Central Bank maintain the current stance of monetary policies without limits and currency wars. The monetary incentives provided to the governments are used for unproductive projects that generate overcapacity and debt, supporting "zombie" companies. The banks are weak and unable to support lending for investments and economic activity. High debt levels lead to higher borrowing costs. The parallel bubbles continue their course and incentivize further gross misallocation of capital. China is unable to float and devalue the CNY in an orderly fashion, which leads to capital outflows and forced more intervention and stimulus, which prevent the restructuring and reform plans, adding to the imbalances. Crude oil and commodity prices sell-off, exposing producer countries across emerging markets. Geopolitical risks materialize. Weaker economic and confidence result in unemployment. Central Banks forced to ease monetary policy further, pushing ahead with helicopter money and new rounds of QE, which is adopted by new countries such as China. Currency wars are back, creating further imbalances and deflation. Debt monetization a possibility, which would lead to major currency devaluation. A period that would be characterized by extreme volatility and much higher gold prices.

The Silent Hero

I hope this book plays the role of the silent hero, the image used by Nicholas Nassim Taleb to describe the actions that avert a crisis that—by definition—would have never happened. In the meantime, I hope the reader will be better prepared to avoid common implementation mistakes and make better and informed decisions.

CHAPTER 8

Bubbles: How to Avoid Them

Benchmarks, The New Partner in Crime

I believe that benchmarks are partially responsible for the current trend in financial inflation. Benchmarks are self-imposed guidelines for investments that in practice act as trend-following mechanisms that are relentlessly following the steps of central bank buying, contributing to the creation of bubbles.

Benchmarks set the expectations for asset allocation and returns, the bar that active investment managers are held against. In principle, investment managers have the discretion to be *overweight, neutral,* or *underweight* relative to what the benchmark dictates, but in practice have quite small discretion for tactical asset allocation decisions, which means that the bulk of the assets will stay invested in the benchmark, regardless of their valuations.

Traditional allocation models seek to mitigate overall portfolio volatility by combining asset classes with low correlations to each other, which has proven to be less stable, with long-term correlations such as globalization driving correlations higher. A dynamic that has been exacerbated by the wave of parallel bubbles that are being created by the monetary policy without limits. This leads to the dangerous and worrying development of false diversification.

Risk and Behavioral Factors

Risk factors can be defined as the underlying drivers of risk exposures and performance. Some of those risk factors are interest rates risk, credit risk, inflation risk, currency risk, and commodity risk. The traditional government bond asset class is therefore broken down into its risk components, namely interest rate, credit, and currency. This risk is then aggregated across all components to provide a better assessment of diversification and volatility.

The investment industry is slowly but steadily moving away from allocations based on *asset classes* to allocations based on *risk factors*. A positive development in my view that will make gold and oil are fundamental building blocks for risk-factor allocations, as they provide unique diversification under certain scenarios, such as inflation risk, duration risk, currency risk, and geopolitical risks.

From Beta to Alpha

Asset allocators looking for ways to reduce their exposure to the wrong asset classes can opt to switch from beta allocations (long-only) to alpha allocations (long/short), which have the potential to participate in further appreciation and simultaneously reduce the downside exposure.

Financial Assets

It is a fact that monetary policy without limits has distorted the valuation of financial assets around the world. The epicenter has been centered on government bonds, but has spread across other credit and equity instruments, benefiting the weakest players (such as high yield or EM) the most.

The asset inflation has had a positive effect on the economy via the *wealth effect* and other inflationary dynamics that I will discuss later under the *Soros Reflexivity* section. A calculated bet from Central Banks that hopes that fundamentals will converge to prices. Over the past few years, the deflationary pressures and the perceived fragility of the recovery (or at least lack of strength) has been an excuse for Central Banks to keep "lower for longer" rates.

The normalization of monetary policy (interest rates going up) is bad news for financial asset valuations and will test the resilience of the underlying fundamentals of the economy as the monetary stimuli are removed.

Real Assets

Faced with low or even negative interest rates and inflated financial assets, investors are looking for alternative investments such as real estate, infrastructure, or timber, among others. These *Real Assets* have benefited indirectly from low borrowing costs, but generally lagged financial asset inflation due to the slack and overcapacity in the system.

Faced with potential hikes and inflationary pressures, will real assets behave like bonds (go down) or benefit from inflation?

The key differentiation is leverage. Real estate markets that are heavily leveraged will likely fall as borrowing costs go up. Real estate markets that are not leveraged will likely hold their value better, and even go up, as monetary inflation kicks in.

Monetary Assets

I would put gold into a different category, called monetary assets, which does not only benefit from inflation but also plays a key role as store of value and in my view is best placed to play the role of ultimate reserve currency of the world. More on this shortly.

CHAPTER 9

Anti-bubbles: How to Profit and Protect the Portfolio via Gold, Volatility, and Correlation

Playing to Make Money, Not to Be Correct

I believe the gold market is at the beginning of a multiyear bull run. A bullish supercycle that offers investors a highly asymmetric risk–reward with "a few *hundred* dollars of downside and a few *thousand* dollars of upside."

First you need to understand the rules of the game.
Then you need to play better than everyone else.

—Albert Einstein

Many respected analysts hold the exact opposite view. They believe that gold prices are going through a quasi-permanent bear market and prices will continue to go down "forever." They have their own perspective and solid arguments to defend their views and investment thesis.

Time will tell who is right and who is wrong but, frankly, it does not matter. Focusing on being correct on our prediction misses the point. What really matters, the real and only true objective of the trading and investment game is to *make money*, not to be correct about our *predictions*.

Many respected analysts and strategists consistently lose money because their objective is to be accurate and correct in their predictions. They lose money because they are playing the game by the wrong rules.

True ignorance is not the absence of knowledge,
but the refusal to acquire it.

—Karl Popper

Let's look at a simple example to explain the difference between "playing to be correct" and "playing to make money." Let's assume that alternative A has a 90 percent chance of making $1 and alternative B has a 10 percent chance of making $100.

If I play the game to be "correct," I should bet for alternative A (I would win 90 percent of the time).

If I play the game to "make money" I should bet for alternative B (expected win = $100 * 10% = $10, much higher than the expected win of alternative A = $1 * 90% = $0.9). It is your choice how you want to play the game. My strong suggestion: play to make money.

Bulls, Bears, and Pigs

The current market consensus is as polarized as ever, and that's why I believe it is going to be a very volatile and bumpy road. The bulls that are hoping for a steady and orderly appreciation of gold may be set for a surprise, and may end up being pigs.

Bulls make money, Bears make money, Pigs get slaughtered.
—Wall Street Saying

Playing to win removes the ego from investment processes. Recognizing and quickly correcting our mistakes is a key trait of successful investors and traders. Being stubborn and slow is a trait of losers. You choose.

You may have noted the extensive use of the word *thesis*. An investment thesis is meant to be tested and either validated or rejected. A mindset that aims to remove our ego from the decision process.

One million positive observations do not prove a theory right.
One negative observation proves a theory wrong.
—Karl Popper

Smart Investing in Gold

There are many ways to invest in the gold market, but just like "not all that glitters is gold," I believe that many gold-related investments will perform poorly and some even have the potential to fail spectacularly.

One of the primary objectives of this book is to educate investors on the alternatives available for gold and volatility investing, and avoid situations of "I was right, but wrong."

Debunking the Myth of Gold Equities

Many investors are currently implementing their gold views via gold mining stocks, also known as gold miners. Some of those investors are buying gold miners based on the *naive* belief that owning gold miners are just like owning physical gold. A misconception in my view that I feel compelled to debunk.

This false belief is strengthened by the fact that many investment vehicles, such as the Blackrock *Gold* Fund, give the wrong impression of investing in gold but in reality are investing in gold mining stocks. I would like to believe that those investing into those funds are doing it with their eyes wide open (knowing they are buying gold miners, and not gold), but I fear it is not always the case. In my view all these funds should be renamed to Blackrock Gold *Mining* Fund to avoid any confusion and potential mis-selling with investors.

Investors must understand that a scenario of much higher gold prices does not necessarily imply much higher gold equity valuations. There are many reasons why the divergence in pricing (known as "basis risk") can arise. I will discuss more of the more relevant ones, but there are many more.

Real Options

One of the best university courses I have taken in my life was taught by Professor Graham Davies, at the Colorado School of Mines, where I completed my Masters in Mineral Economics. The course introduced me to the concept of real options and forever changed the way I looked at the world.

> *A lettuce is the right, but not the obligation, to make yourself a salad.*
>
> —Professor Graham Davies, Colorado School of Mines

I followed my passion for the topic of Real Options theory and completed my thesis on its application to Mineral Asset valuation. Traditional models relied on discounted cash flows and sensitivity analysis, which I found very limited. The Real Option framework viewed and valued the assets as the *right*, but *not the obligation*, to extract the reserves on the ground. The mine could be valued using the models used for financial options, such as Black and Scholes, using the forward curve, the volatility of the price, the Strike Price as the Marginal Cost of Production, or the Option Expiry as the time given by the license. A framework that opened enormous possibilities.

Taxation, Expropriation, and Nationalization

Gold mining companies tend to operate in a range of geographical locations and jurisdictions, which I will refer to as "host governments." The probability that a host government will *tax* your revenues, *expropriate* your gold mining assets, or even outright *nationalize* the company, increases *exponentially* with the gold price.

Think about what would happen to your gold mining assets in "Emerging Market country X" (I won't name names, but there are multiple examples across all continents, not just the usual suspects in Africa and Latin America) if a mega bullish gold price scenario. Thank you very much.

Host governments are also driven by populist measures. "Foreign multinationals are coming and taking our precious assets." Rings the bell.

It is therefore not inconceivable that at record high gold prices the equity valuation of those gold assets would be a big fat zero.

Up and Out Calls

For those versed in exotic derivatives, I would describe gold equities as an "up and out call" on gold, which describes a "knock-out" feature if gold prices reach a certain price substantially *above* the current market.

Jurisdiction

The dynamics described previously are very much a function of the jurisdictional risk of the assets, more than the listing of the company, which also matters. In that sense, we may gain a false sense of security from investing in a Canadian-listed miner, but if the assets are all in some dubious sub-Saharan Africa, the valuation should reflect those risks.

Marginal Cost of Production

Let's now think about the exact opposite scenario. Prices have collapsed to new historical lows, a price that is very significantly below the average marginal cost of production in the industry. Under this extreme price scenario, the higher marginal cost producers would be burning cash and would eventually be forced to shut down, effectively reducing the supply.

For all commodities that are produced and consumed, such as oil or corn, the supply destruction would eat into inventories ,which, once depleted, would incentivise substitution and destroy demand via high prices. The price elasticity of demand would determine how high prices need to go in order to destroy the necessary demand. In turn, higher prices provide an incentive for producers to return to the market and increase supply. These dynamics, driven by Adam Smith's invisible hand, provide a strong floor at the marginal cost of production for these commodities.

But gold is not a normal commodity. In fact, some respected research houses don't even consider gold as a commodity at all. The rationale is that all the gold ever-mined is currently sitting somewhere in the form of "above ground stocks." In the oil market, the "above ground stocks" are measured in days of consumption. In the gold market, it would be decades.

The key implication is that the marginal cost of production is not a solid floor for gold prices. That is, gold prices could, in principle, trade substantially below the marginal cost of production for substantially long periods of time. Bad news for producers and their equity valuations.

Down and Out Calls

The mirror image of the "up and out call" described previously, whereby for those versed in exotic derivatives, I would add to my description of gold equities the "down and out feature," which describes a "knock-out" feature if gold prices sustain a certain price *below* the current market.

Hedging

In order to protect their cash flows and equity valuations, many gold producers have historically engaged in *hedging*, whereby they lock-in a minimum selling price for a portion of their future production.

Hedging programs are meant to be risk-reducing, but that's not always the case. It is important for investors in gold mining stocks to understand the hedging policy in *full* detail. I will describe some of the common mistakes and hidden risks so investors can make more informed decisions.

The simplest and most conservative hedging strategy is to price gold price insurance via *vanilla put options*. The producer pays a premium to *protect* itself against lower prices while retaining full *participation* to higher prices, as the investor is effectively long a synthetic call option. The worst-case scenario is the loss of premium, which would only happen if prices are higher. A happy scenario for the gold producer. This is my preferred hedging strategy by far.

Other producers are reluctant to pay an upfront premium. Instead, they engage in "zero premium" strategies such as forward sales or zero-premium option strategies that provide some degree of *downside protection* but commit some degree of *upside participation*.

It is critical to understand the credit terms of these hedging facilities. Those hedging programs supported by open lines of credit are fine. But those programs subject to margin calls create a very dangerous, often fatal, dynamic. Let me explain.

Let's say a gold miner has 10 million ounces of proven reserves, which he hopes to extract over 10 years at a regular pace of 1 million ounces per year. Let's assume that he has limited cash and decides to hedge 50 percent of the production (500,000 oz per year) at the then prevailing forward prices. If the gold price sells-off, the mark-to-market value of his hedging program is positive. On the other hand, if the price rallies, the mark-to-market of his hedging program will be negative. Let's assume that the gold price is rallied by $100/oz from the initial hedging price. In that case, the mark-to-market loss of the program will be $100/oz multiplied by 50,000 oz/year over 10 years equals $5m mark-to-market loss. In principle, these losses are offset against gains of the gold underground. Hedge accounting forces the companies to represent these gains or losses in their balance sheet. So far, so good. The problem emerges if the hedging program was subject to margin calls. In that instance, the bank will require the producer to *post* the full mark-to-market ($5m in this example) in cash. Very often, the producer does not have that cash at hand or needs it to run its operations. In order to pay for the margin, the company is forced to borrow money, which in some instances may be both challenging and expensive. As an old colleague would say, "excess liquidity has never made anyone insolvent." The opposite unfortunately often holds true, and lack of liquidity can lead to the bankruptcy of perfectly solvent businesses.

Finally, other producers prefer to collect upfront premium. They engage in strategies such as call granting strategies or exotic strategies with complex conditions, which are difficult to price and manage. In some cases, ill-designed hedging programs have created dynamics where the producer was net short the underlying. Over my two decade career, I have seen many of these programs blow up spectacularly due to a combination of leverage, currency, and exotic risks. The Australian miners or Ashanti Goldfields spring to mind.

Even well-designed hedging programs can create conflicts. By construction, a positive outcome of the hedging program is not in the best interest of the company. And vice versa, a negative outcome of the hedging program, which should be in the best interest of the company, is not necessarily always in the best of the finance department in charge of it. Badly run companies are not clear in their objectives and often play the blame game after the fact. The typical 20/20 hindsight, "I told you not to hedge. We have lost/wasted X million $." A dynamic I refer to as "which team are you rooting for? Do you want prices to go up, or go down?" A dynamic that, believe it or not, is more often the rule than the exception.

The gold market has historically been divided into two philosophical camps: the hedgers and the nonhedgers. During bear markets the hedgers tend to do better and vice versa, the nonhedgers do better during bull markets.

A well-designed hedging policy can significantly reduce the "down and out" risk, but both hedgers and nonhedgers are subject to the "up and out" knockout feature, and that's why the jurisdiction is such an important consideration when investing in gold equities.

Exploration, Juniors, Majors

The stage of development and the strength of the balance sheet are major considerations when investing in gold miners. The framework of Real Option can be very helpful to understand the risk and behavior of the underlying. The detail of the discussion are beyond the purpose of this book, but the key point I want to stress is that the more "non-gold" risks that we add to the equation, the greater the risk for a "I was right, but wrong" type of outcome.

Management

Another important source of optionality and basis risk is the quality of the management of the mining company. They are the ones who take the strategic and tactical decisions in terms of organic expansion versus M&A, hedging, and many other important considerations that can result in the success or failure of companies.

Gold Equities Are Not Gold

In summary, I am not saying that gold equities are better or worse investments than gold. What I am saying is that they are *different*. Those investors who are investing in gold based on the macro topics discussed in this book should be very aware of the large basis risk they may be incurring by investing in gold equities.

At this point in time, many gold equities are behaving as highly leveraged positively correlated assets to gold prices, but those relationships can and will change over time. Leverage can be achieved via many other ways.

Correlations can break for many reasons, and why I recommend that gold equities are viewed primarily as equity investments, and not as gold investments. You need to know what you are buying: the quality of the reserves, the jurisdiction, the management, the leverage, the financing, the taxation, and many other important factors that drive the price in addition to gold prices.

Most investors understand that oil futures are different from BP or Shell. I hope the brief and simple discussion earlier will open the eyes of gold investors too.

Gold Services

There are many other creative ways in which investors can implement their views. A good friend of mine has bought gold drilling equipment in Africa. The view is that gold drilling rates are positively correlated to gold prices. They are real options (the right but not the obligation to drill). Investing in the gold services industry worked very well for someone named Levi Strauss during the gold rush of the 1800s.

Lessons from the Oil Market

Investors in gold miners should pay close attention to the lessons learnt from the recent bull market in energy markets where many investors were correct in their bullish outlook but gold prices but lost money due to the wrong implementation.

Production sharing agreements reached taxation levels of 99 percent in some cases, which effectively converted equity investments, theoretically call options, into put options with limited upside and full unlimited downside. Not what many investors thought they were buying into. Another case of the dreadful "I was right, but wrong" we are trying to avoid here.

The "Widow-Maker"

Another important lesson to be learnt from the oil market is the dangers in Relative Value trading ("RV") between oil and oil equities.

The run-up in oil prices from 2005 to the peak of 2008 was characterized by a major divergence between the oil futures curve (which was updated live) and the assumptions used by oil equity analysts (which were very stale, and significantly lagging the rapid moves in the oil futures curve).

Many investors were monitoring the divergence in implied valuations between oil equities (which implied $40/bbl oil) and oil futures (which implied $60/bbl). A 50 percent premium that enticed investors to buy oil equities and sell oil futures.

Such convergence plays can be implemented in many ways. One is on a "dollar neutral basis," whereby you buy $100 of oil equities and sell $100 of oil to hedge it. A dollar neutral implementation assumes that oil equities have an oil beta (sensitivity) of 100 percent, which is pretty much never the case. It also assumes that the volatility of both assets is the same, which is not necessarily true either. As a result, convergence plays tend to be implemented on a "beta neutral" or "volatility neutral" basis.

To the pain and surprise of many, the valuation spread continued to wide rapidly as oil prices rallied, creating large mark-to-market losses in the oil futures, which required additional margin, while the oil equities were lagging behind unable and unwilling to catch up.

The divergence reached such extremes that the trade was commonly known as a "widow maker."

In some cases, the perception of low risk due to the high positive correlations led investors to implement their bets in large notional sizes. A very common and potentially fatal mistake, in relative value trading, which I have seen many times over the years, such as Brent versus West Texas Intermediate ("WTI"), or Gold versus Silver, assets that tend to show positive correlation but occasionally show negative correlation, leaving investors with wild swings and often large losses.

A risk I call "correlation breakout," a very real possibility for gold and gold equities, especially at very high gold prices, due to the risk of taxation, expropriation, and nationalization.

Debunking the Myth of Physical Gold

Many investors are currently implementing their gold views via physical gold only. I totally agree with the merits of physical gold (its physical and chemical properties are what makes gold unique), but I think it is worth reviewing some of the common and potentially dangerous misconceptions associated with physical and paper.

The Rationale for Physical Gold

There are many instances when physical gold may well be the most effective and appropriate way to implement a gold investment. There are many others when it may not.

Many investors buy physical gold to take it "off the system." They have gold in private storage facilities, outside of the radar of banks and governments. Gold has played a key role as money since inception, but has experienced a progressive detachment, starting with seigniorage (gold coins issued by the government), paper money (fiat currency), the digitalization of money (credit cards), the virtualization of money (bitcoin), and more recently negative interest rates ("tax on cash"), which are in my view planting the seeds of a monetary supercycle that may bring gold back to the monetary scene. More on this later.

Many investors also buy physical gold because of its convenience yield. History is full of examples of families forced to flee their homes and leave behind their land and possessions, but were able to take their gold (ingots, coins, jewelry, etc.), giving them a clear head-start to rebuild their lives somewhere else.

All these benefits come at a cost in the form of storage cost, insurance cost, lower liquidity, which need to be balanced with the benefits and the ultimate goal of holding gold, which leads me to the discussion about the end game.

Paying with Gold Coins in the Supermarket?

Let's assume for a second that gold has regained its status in the monetary scene. Does it mean that we will be paying in the supermarket with gold coins? No, we won't. Does that mean that the USD or the EUR or the JPY will disappear? No, they won't. In my view fiat currencies will continue to be used after a monetary supercycle.

What will be different is the value of those fiat currencies relative to gold. Instead of buying a Fiat 1 with your gold, you may be able to buy a Ferrari, who knows.

The ultimate goal of owning gold is to preserve value and exchange it for something else at a future day. A holiday, a meal, a house, whatever that is, in my view it will be cheaper in gold terms in the future. As a result, the objective is to find ways within the system that preserve the value of our savings.

Mind the Basis

I have come across some passionate gold bugs who believe paper-gold is worthless. They proposed a strategy that would buy physical gold and simultaneously sell gold futures (paper-gold). The rationale, they argued, was that paper-gold was not backed by sufficient physical gold, and as a result, in their view, physical gold should be worth more than paper gold: a very basic and possibly lethal mistake. Let me explain via an example.

Let's assume that there are 1 million ounces of gold and open interest of 100 million ounces of gold futures. What would happen if the people holding the 100 million ounces of longs decided to take physical delivery with a fairly short notice? Clearly, the amount of physical gold is not sufficient to deliver into the obligations, which forces the short positions to cover their position and potentially pay a significant premium above the then prevailing physical gold price. In the commodity lingo, gold would turn into a steep *backwardation*, which reflects the premium for immediate availability. As a result, those holding the short futures and long physical would incur very sizeable losses. A dynamic that bears some similarities with the Sumitomo scandal, when in 1995, the chief copper trader at Sumitomo, Yasuo Hamanaka, tried to corner the market but ended up costing Sumitomo over $1.8b in trading losses and a suspension of 10 years.

Gold ETF

The gold ETF (Exchange Traded Fund) was a game changer for the gold market. For the first time ever, retail and institutional investors alike, would be able to buy physical gold as easily as they could buy shares of Microsoft.

The concept was very simple. Create a company whose assets are only gold, say 100 oz, and its liabilities is only equity, say 100 shares. By construction, the share price of that company would equate the price of gold on a one-by-one basis. The ETF would carry a management fee (not negligible 0.50 percent p.a.) to pay for the cost of storage, insurance, and operations.

The liquidity has grown significantly over the years and has already surpassed the liquidity of the Over the Counter ("OTC") market, where all the gold trading used to happen.

Many people are critical of the second-order and third-order risks incurred when buying an ETF, such as the force majeure clause, which may lead to cash settlement (at the then prevailing prices), which in my personal view is a minor risk. Personally, I am more worried about the risks involved in gold equities or the wrong type of physical trading than the risks of ETFs.

Gold Futures

Moving on to leveraged investments (so far gold equities, physical gold, and gold ETF tend to be "fully funded" investments), gold futures allow investors to express bullish and bearish views with significant leverage.

The initial margin is the amount we must deposit with the exchange to cover for potential losses. The margin varies with the underlying and can also change over time based on the liquidity and volatility of the market.

Assuming an initial margin of 10 percent, investors are able to take risk on much larger positions (in principle up to 10 times larger in this case), which is why speculators favor futures versus fully funded vehicles.

Gold Structured Products

Many investors implement gold via structured products sold via private banks and financial advisors. These strategies tend to be optically very attractive but carry several layers of structuring and distribution fees that dramatically reduce the attractiveness and risk–reward of these products.

My father has a saying that goes something like "meat in a sock, for whoever stocked it," which tries to explain that when you have a steak you can see the type of meat you are eating, but when you eat a sausage as you don't know what meat is inside.

Let's start with the *Principal Protected* or *Capital Guaranteed* products. These products are composed from two parts: the zero-coupon bond and the option.

The zero coupon bond is the portion of the capital that we need to invest day one in order to receive $100 at maturity. Oversimplifying, if the issuer is willing to pay 5 percent for one year, we would only need to invest approximately $95.23 for one year, and receive 95.23 * 1.05 = 100 at maturity. The higher the interest rate, the less we need to invest day one. The longer the maturity, the less we need to invest day one.

The option is generally some kind of insurance product, whereby we invest the balance between the amount paid by the investor ($100) in this case, minus the commissions (can be several percent points, let's assume 1 percent for the structurer and 1 percent for the distributor), which would leave us with just 2.76% (= 100% – 95.23% – 1% – 1%) to buy something.

In order to make the structured products optically attractive, the banks often add a few bells and whistles such as knockouts and other exotic features that add leverage and reduce the probability of success. Not a very effective way to express a view.

The main problem with structured products is that the return of the capital is guaranteed by the *issuer* of the note. If your issuer goes bankrupt, the note will be worthless, irrespective of what happened to the gold option. Not an acceptable risk for most gold investors, who are trying to protect themselves from systemic risks.

As a result, I would not recommend gold structured products in general unless we have a very clear understanding of what it is inside, the risks, and the pricing, in which they can be effective packages. Otherwise, I can think of many more effective ways to implement your gold views.

Mind the Leverage

Financial leverage is possibly the number one reason most investors suffer from "I was right, but wrong" type of mistakes.

Physical investments tend to be the most "sticky," and often last for many years. Gold ETF investments are reasonably sticky, as investors can hold to their views without having to worry about margin calls. Gold futures, on the other hand, tend to see wild swings in open interest and positions.

Trend Following Strategies

I often come across investors who tell me, "yes, I own gold via CTAs," which in my view has some merits but has the potential to fall in the "I was right, but wrong" category. Many reasons why, but first and foremost because Commodity Trade Advisors ("CTA") try to catch trends in both directions and therefore buy and *sell* gold, which often puts them in the opposite direction to where you expect them to be.

There are certain scenarios where trend following strategies work very well (clear trend with low volatility) and other scenarios when trend following strategies fail spectacularly (no clear trend and high volatility). My big picture view of higher volatility and dislocations does not favor CTAs.

Discretionary Macro Strategies

I often come across investors who tell me that they are long gold via discretionary macro strategies. Similar to CTAs, however, global macro managers can play gold from the long and short side. Currently, the investment community is highly polarized. Some managers are very bullish, and some managers may be very bearish. That's in principle a good thing as we know where they stand, but macro managers are also known for changing their views and positions quite quickly.

Even dedicated commodity hedge funds, which many investors expect to have a long bias, have been caught many times short the commodity. A very painful experience for the investor, and yet another case of "I was right, but wrong" in the gold market.

Silver, Platinum, and Palladium

Silver has played a key monetary role throughout history. In Spanish, "plata," is used today to refer to money in countries such as Argentina. Some Central Banks, such as Russia, still hold silver as part of their FX reserves, but they are the exception rather than the rule.

There are several reasons why silver will play a less critical role than gold in a Gold Perfect Storm and Monetary Supercycle scenario. To start, silver's chemical properties are not as noble as gold, as silver easily oxidizes and produces a blackish coat we must regularly polish. Silver is also more reactive and can be attacked by acids that gold is resistant to. Lastly, the relative scarcity and price makes silver a less efficient store of value. Based on current ratios, we would need 70 times more volume of silver than gold to store a given amount of USD.

Platinum and palladium are precious metals with extensive investment and industrial use. Historically they have played a minor role as monetary assets, but their properties and scarcity make them solid candidates as a store of value, to the point that platinum prices have historically traded at a premium to gold. The concentration of mining supply (platinum is mainly produced in South Africa, and palladium in Russia) has important implications as currency fluctuations in the South African Rand ("ZAR") and the Russian Ruble ("RUB") are a key driver of these metals.

Overall, the relationship across the main four precious metals offers attractive relative value opportunities, and I have historically actively traded the main ratios gold/silver, platinum/gold, and platinum/palladium.

Smart Gold

The Gold Perfect Storm investment thesis is not just about gold. It is a thesis about bubbles and anti-bubbles, where gold, volatility, and correlation will all play a very relevant role.

Based on the Gold Perfect Storm investment thesis and the experience I have gained trading and managing risk over the past two decades, I have perfected a strategy that I call Smart Gold.

The strategy has four building blocks, each one addressing a set of opportunities and risks.

Building Block #1: Long Gold

Smart Gold invests in gold only, not in gold equities, and is designed to provide investors with an effective vehicle for Strategic Allocations to Gold, which is supported by both traditional asset allocation models (such as Markowitz) and modern approaches based on risk-factors.

As a risk-factor, gold is a unique asset class that combines three distinct characteristics, namely (i) gold as a commodity, (ii) gold as a currency/monetary asset, (iii) gold as a credit/safe haven asset that make it an unique diversifier and insurance against many of the key risks ahead, namely inflation, duration, credit, equity, inflation, geopolitics, currency, among other direct implications of the Lehman Squared and the Gold Perfect Storm investment theses.

In addition to its strategic nature, the tactical case for gold is also very supportive (in my view gold offers a few *hundred* dollars of downside and a few *thousand* dollars of upside), and possibly even more asymmetric in most non-USD currencies, and believe that the current global market conditions are setting the beginning of a multiyear bull cycle as we Central Banks, Governments, and market participants are (1) testing the limits of monetary policy, (2) testing the limits of credit and equity markets, which will eventually lead to (3) testing the limits of fiat currencies.

Another common objection that comes up is "gold has no yield." Indeed, in a yield-seeking environment, the negative carry of physical gold (storage and insurance costs) has contributed to gold's anti-bubble dynamics. The yield-seeking bubble inflating fixed income, credit, equity, high yield, Emerging Markets ("EM"), and so on, has a mirror image in gold and volatility. A dynamic that I believe will eventually reverse leaving investors focused on the return *of* their capital, instead of return *on* their capital.

In this context, gold has become a real alternative to negative yielding cash and bonds, which make gold a "positive carry" versus trillions of cash and bonds in Euros ("EUR") and Japanese Yen ("JPY"). Time will tell how much damage has been created during the "yield seeking bubble" created, but the downside risks in my view are highly asymmetric.

Building Block #2: Long Gold Volatility

Smart Gold buys gold price insurance based on both quantitative and qualitative factors.

I believe that implied volatility is deflated due to the combination of the Central Bank Put and the Complacent Desperate search for yield. From a quantitative perspective, I seek to capture relative value from the divergence in *implied* versus *realized* volatility. From a qualitative perspective, I seek to capture relative value from the divergence in *implied* versus *expected* volatility. On a historical basis, Smart Gold has been a consistent buyer of short-dated gold volatility, where the most attractive risk–reward has been, but it is also able to buy longer dated volatility to take advantage of cheap vega and to benefit from the trend in volatility.

The gold insurance overlay addresses one important consideration often raised by investors: "gold's volatility is too high for me." Smart Gold long insurance profile is designed to reduce the "bad volatility" (to the downside) via long gold puts, and maintain "good volatility" (to the upside), effectively resulting in realized volatility that—by construction—will notably be lower than gold.

Smart Gold is designed to provide "blue sky" exposure to gold prices, which is achieved through its long-bias approach to insurance. In my opinion, yield-seeking strategies such as *covered calls* are negating the benefits of holding gold on the first place.

Another major benefit of Smart Gold is that it is focused on the long-run, and removes concerns about entry and exit, which are extremely difficult to time. By embracing volatility (instead of resist or fight it) Smart Gold aims to act as a "gold accumulation" program, reinvesting the proceeds from insurance to buy more gold without any incremental cash outlay, thus benefiting from both rallies and selloffs.

This is important as many investors are disillusioned with gold, having suffered significant capital losses and dilution over the past few years. From the highs of 2012 to the lows of December 2015, gold collapsed by almost 50 percent and the gold miners by almost 80 percent, leaving a sour taste to investors. Many of them sold along the way down, locking-in losses. Smart Gold is designed to enhance capital preservation via the purchase of gold price insurance.

By adding a long insurance profile, Smart Gold enjoys the benefits of a long-only strategy (known behavior as risk factor for asset allocation) but also the benefits of absolute return (capital preservation and higher risk-adjusted returns).

Building Block #3: Rotation Across Precious Metals

Smart Gold rotates a portion of its gold exposure into other precious metals, namely silver, platinum, and palladium.

The rationale is to capture "mean reverting" relative value opportunities that complement the "breakout" profile of the long insurance.

Building Block #4: Long Tail Risk

Smart Gold deploys a small portion of its capital to buy tail risk insurance in option format.

The idea is to take advantage of the low implied volatility and high implied correlations. Historically, the strategy has bought options that believe gold will go higher and Euro would go lower, a scenario that the market believes as unlikely due to the recent high realized correlation between the non-USD currencies, including gold.

At the time of writing, the market holds the view that gold and the Japanese Yen are "the same thing," and are trading at similar level of implied volatility and with high realized correlation. This dynamic offers an attractive contrarian opportunity to buy options that would make money if gold trades higher and the yen simultaneously trades lower. These transactions can offer extremely high risk–reward (20 to 1 or higher).

At the time of writing, gold remains a contrarian view versus the complacency of global markets who believe we can "*print* and *borrow* our way out of a problem." Smart Gold is positioned to participate in the long-term appreciation of gold, while embracing and taking advantage of the short-term volatility, short-term dislocations, correlation breakouts, and tail-risk events.

Contrarian Bias

Smart Gold has a contrarian bias, which means it favors views that go against the consensus and speculative position of the market. The main benefit of contrarian ideas is that they have superior risk–reward than consensus "*me too*" ideas. The main consideration is that contrarian ideas tend to go against the prevailing trend and, as Keynes famously said, "the market can remain irrational for longer than I can remain solvent."

The consensus and positioning can be monitored via public information such as the Commodity Futures Trading Commission ("CFTC") reports. In addition, I also pay close attention to expressions such as "it's a no brainer" or "it should be higher." In my experience can be a red flag for market imbalances.

I favor contrarian trades but also invest in ideas that are *neutral* or *in-line* with the market consensus when other sources of asymmetry offer sufficiently attractive risk–reward.

I rarely invest in ideas that are *crowded*, and when I do invest, it is because it is a long-term theme I want to stay invested in, as it has been the case in gold, and I look for ways to protect my position and take advantage of short-term dislocations, often via relative value and insurance. I call this Smart Beta. More on this later.

Investment Horizon

The investment horizon of my Gold Perfect Storm thesis is three to five years. I have a reasonably high degree of conviction that gold will be much higher than today against most currencies, including the U.S. dollar.

The investment horizon for a normalization of volatility is shorter. Realized volatility has notably picked up since Brexit and the U.S. elections and in my view may have already bottomed.

In terms of implementation, it is important to ensure that the instruments and leverage are adequate for our investment horizon. As a rule, the higher the leverage the more likely to be taken out of our position by corrections and noise. A dynamic that could result in the unfortunate "I was right, but wrong," because at the end of the day, being early is another way of being wrong.

Timing

It is impossible to time the market perfectly all the time. Sometimes we are too early. Sometimes we are too late. Sometimes we are just on time. Just like catching the bus.

Most amateur investors focus only on the *entry* and totally the *exit*. As the market saying goes "you make and lose money when you exit, not when you enter."

I recently read a book titled *The Art of Execution* by Lee Freeman-Schorr, which puts forward a simple and clear framework for best and worst practices for entries and exits. The book analyzes behavior when we are losing money and when we are making money, and creates personality traits for each behavior. Lee identifies the "rabbit" (lets losses run), the "hunter" (adds to losing positions), the "assassin" (cuts losses quickly), the "raider" (takes quick profits), and the "connoisseur" (lets profits run). I have adapted that framework slightly, and prefer to analyze behavior as a function of entries and exits, which opens up a new hidden personality trait, I have called "the collector" (adds to winning positions).

There are multiple combinations for entry and exit. The worst possible combination is a *rabbit* when we are losing and a raider when we are winning. Failure guaranteed.

Luck versus Skill

In the short term, luck is king. The component of "noise" in the price dominates. The probability of heads in one fair coin toss is 50 percent.

In the long term, skill is king. The component of "noise" evens out and becomes negligible. The probability of having 10 consecutive heads is 0.1 percent.

As a corollary, there is little point in fundamental investing with the expectation of making money in the short term. In the short term, pretty much anything can happen; bad players can win and good players can lose.

Path Dependency

Over the years I have learnt to embrace—rather than resist—the irrationality of the market. *Eventually* being right can make you feel good, but it is not the objective of the investment game, as we discussed. The only true objective is to *make money*. Full stop. With that in mind, our analysis and implementation must incorporate nonfundamental considerations such as speculative positioning, which can be a dangerous source of volatility and risk.

First Mover Advantage

I finished cowriting my first book, *The Energy World is Flat: Opportunities from the end of Peak Oil* in March 2014, when crude oil was comfortable trading above $100/bbl and the belief in the Peak Oil theory was very much accepted.

Our investment thesis, "Flattening of the Energy World," presented a transformational framework that challenged many of the fundamental beliefs then prevailing in the energy market, that would invariably lead to the collapse of crude oil prices, the natural gas glut, the collapse in LNG prices, the emergence of the "energy broadband" (a global network of land and "floating pipelines" in the form of LNG infrastructure), and the end of crude oil's monopoly in transportation demand, among other concepts and contrarian conclusions.

The chapter titled "the Btu that broke OPEC's back" (adaptation of "the straw that broke the camel's back") challenged the belief that the "Central Bank of Oil" was in full control. A dynamic that has important similarities with the current belief (in my view misconception) that Central Banks are infallible. More on this later.

The timing was impossible to predict with certainty, but in our view "the collapse of crude oil prices was a matter of when, and not a matter of if." The unavoidable consequence of severe imbalances. A situation that is repeating itself today in other parts of the economy and global markets.

As a first mover challenging the status quo, our ideas and investment thesis were received with great skepticism, almost like *science fiction*. Not anymore.

To our credit, the investment thesis of the *Flattening of the Energy World* has not only been validated, but actually strengthened, with the phenomenal stress tests it has had to endure over the past almost three years. The *Flattening of the Energy World* is today very much alive and kicking, and has been a useful tool to anticipate and rationale the behavior from OPEC (as per my interview in Real Vision TV published in January 2017). But "that will be another story that will be told another time," as Michael Ende's *Never-ending Story* used to finish each chapter.

The investment theses that I present in this book, "Lehman Squared" and "Gold's Perfect Storm" reached global distribution with the article published on the front page of the *Financial Times* on August 8, 2016, but the ideas were first presented on a large public scale in October 2015 during the annual LBMA Gold Conference in Vienna, where I was part of an investor panel moderated by John Authers, the columnist from the *Financial Times*.

Winning by Not Losing

Capital preservation should be the primary objective of any strategy, and that's why even the long-only strategies I run tend to have a long-only insurance overlay, whereby I buy protection against lower prices at the expense of paying a premium.

> *There are only two rules in investments.*
> *First, never lose money.*
> *Second, never forget lose number one.*
>
> —Warren Buffett

Known Unknowns and Unknown Unknowns

There are many known risks, such as geopolitics, and many unknown risks, such as a global pandemic, that could dramatically change global markets overnight.

Smart Gold long insurance bias (it only buys options, never sells them) is an important risk management tool against any known and unknown unknowns as the worst-case scenario is the loss of initial premium, which is controlled by our risk limits. In the current environment, more than ever, I suggest extreme caution and ensure that, by construction, our portfolio will be able to withstand any shocks, no matter how large or unexpected.

False Diversification

During normal market conditions many asset prices move independently, uncorrelated from each other. During time of stress, however, correlations tend to converge to either +1 or –1.

> *Wide diversification is only required*
> *when investors do not fully understand*
> *the risks they may be incurring.*
>
> —Warren Buffett

During the Lehman crisis most asset classes collapsed at the same time, eroding any expected diversification and correlation benefits one might expect, a phenomenon we could describe as false diversification.

Mind the Gap

Another major consideration is liquidity. The accumulation of large over-valued positions should be a major consideration to anyone involved in those markets. The perception of liquidity during normal market conditions could dry up during times of stress. A problem compounded by the increase in volatility and correlation, which would force investors to liquidate greater and greater sizes at a time of thinner and thinner liquidity.

CHAPTER 10

Conclusion

We are living in extraordinary times. The next few months and years will witness and confirm whether an unprecedented monetary expansion without limits imposed by Central Banks and the subsequent desperate search for yield and a credit expansion without limits will go down in history as a stroke of genius or a reckless gamble.

To start my brief concluding remarks, I would like to give the necessary credit to the Central Banks for their bold and decisive actions during the Global Financial Crisis of 2008 and the European Government Bond Crisis of 2012. Borrowing the words form Mohamed El-Erian "Central Banks, acting boldly and innovatively in the midst of the massive financial crisis, helped the world avert a multi-year depression that would have wreaked havoc on our generation and that of our children." I could not agree more.

At the same time, and perhaps victims of their own success, the Central Banks and Governments have in my view gone too far in their actions and experiments. Currency wars and contagious monetary policy have pushed us in a spiral that is testing the limits of monetary policy, pushing us into the uncharted territory of money printing, negative interest rates, and beyond. The success of these measures reinforced the perception that Central Banks are infallible and in full control, feeding a beast called complacency that ignores risks, rewards speculation, and exacerbates global imbalances.

At the time of writing, it is widely accepted that the collective actions of the Central Banks and Governments have contributed to the distortion of financial asset valuations across global markets. Asset prices would not be where they are without their aggressive intervention. Time will tell if the hefty prices of global bonds and equities are a fair reflection and anticipation of a solid and durable economic recovery—which we all hope and wish for—or a grossly distorted view of reality and expectations for future growth.

Whatever happens, it is also clear that this process of financial asset inflation has been fully intentional. Central Banks set and kept interest rates and government bond yields into unchartered territory by choice, undoubtedly influencing the decisions and actions of lenders and borrowers.

The lenders, faced with the need to generate income, have been forced to lend for longer maturities, to weaker credits, and for lower yields, often incurring excessive and undesired leverage.

The borrowers have taken advantage of this tsunami of cheap and free money. In some cases, the additional debt incurred will be deployed in good investments, in some cases in marginal investments, and in some cases in bad speculative investments that generate overcapacity, misallocate capital and, of course, build bubbles. Time will tell how much damage has been done.

The current dynamic faces an additional problem; a conflict of interest between Central Banks' priorities. On the one hand, to ensure financial stability, in my view their main mandate. On the other hand, to generate employment and economic growth, important, but always within the boundaries of financial stability. The structural deflationary pressures that result from globalization, overcapacity, or the Flattening of the Energy World, among others, have given the Central Banks the comfort to push full steam ahead in their monetary expansion. But beyond the optical illusion of deflation, the second- and third-order effects that are inflating asset valuations may burst back into an even greater deflationary spiral. A dangerous and delicate balance that may be fueling one of the greatest bubbles in financial history. A dynamic that makes me wonder "who polices the police."

The complacent belief that Central Banks are infallible and in full control is at the core of the surge in financial asset valuations, perception of low risk, and surge in structural leverage. Time will tell if the belief will be confirmed or will become a misconception, but the current polarization of views across market participants is a clear indication in my view that the twilight period—where both beliefs and misconceptions co-exist—has already started.

At the time of writing, an overwhelming majority of the market is accepting the beliefs that support current valuations with full complacency, without questioning or understanding the risks they are taking. A small minority, which includes myself, holds the opposite view and challenges these beliefs as misconceptions. Time, as is always the case, will tell.

The timing for a potential bust is unknown—and, who knows, it may never happen—but there are many catalysts lurking in the background that could trigger and accelerate the transformation of beliefs into misconceptions.

Unlike previous crises, the enormous size and global scope of the distortions in asset valuations and misallocations poses risks that are dramatically larger than anything we may have seen in the past: a Lehman Squared scenario, as I call it.

The anti-bubbles—assets that are artificially deflated by misconceptions—such as gold, implied volatility, and implied correlations, have the potential to be both attractive value investments and hedges against financial bubbles.

Yet, as Winston Churchill told us "Success is not final. Failure is not fatal. It is the courage to continue that counts," because whatever the outcome, whoever the winners and losers ahead of us, life will go on. Yet, I hope the ideas and framework presented in this book will help you avoid the dangers and capture the opportunities ahead of us. Help you both win by winning, and help you win by not losing.

I know this final comment may sound strange, but please trust me when I say that I sincerely hope my fears and investment thesis of Lehman Squared and Gold's Perfect Storm will be proven wrong. Being correct in my predictions would not be a happy outcome for the world. The asymmetry and size of the risks are just too large to ignore. As Benjamin Franklin wisely taught us, "if we fail to prepare, we should prepare to fail." I suggest we better prepare. Anti-bubble.

Author Biography

Diego Parrilla is Managing Partner at Quadriga Asset Managers in Madrid, where he brings two decades of investment and senior leadership experience at leading global investment banks and macro hedge funds in London, New York, and Singapore.

Prior to relocating to Spain in 2017, Diego lived in Singapore since 2009, where he worked for leading global macro hedge funds Dymon Asia Capital and BlueCrest Capital Management, and was the founder and Chief Investment Officer of start-up asset manager Natural Resources and Commodity Advisors. Prior to moving to the buy side in 2011, Diego worked for global leading investment banks Merrill Lynch, Goldman Sachs, and JP Morgan, where he held a series of senior leadership roles such as Managing Director and Head of Commodities Asia Pacific, Global Head of Commodity Sales and Structuring, and served as Member of the Management Committee for Global Markets, Global Commodities, and Global Sales at Merrill Lynch and, amongst other external contributions, represented Goldman Sachs in the Management Committee of the London Bullion Market Association ("LBMA"). Diego started his career at JP Morgan in London in 1998 as a Trader of Precious Metals and Foreign Exchange derivatives, where he completed the prestigious JP Morgan Financial Markets training program in NYC.

In addition to his experience as a risk manager and solution provider, Diego is a respected macro commodity analyst and strategist, as co-author with Daniel Lacalle of best-selling "The Energy World is Flat: Opportunities from the End of Peak Oil" (Wiley), which was translated into Spanish as "La Madre De Todas Las Batallas" (Deusto 2014), which was finalist Best Business Book of the year in Spain and has been published in Chinese in 2017. Diego is also a guest contributor to the Financial Times with two recent contributions to the prestigious Insight Column via "The Energy World is Flat" and "Gold's Perfect Storm", where the latter published on the front-page of the written edition 8th Aug 2016. Diego has his own regular column called "Materia Prima" at leading Spanish newspaper El Mundo, and has been a selective guest contributor to other media, such as CNN en Español, CNBC Squawk Box, Real Vision TV, and Bloomberg TV, amongst others. Diego is also passionate about teaching and academia and has been a guest lecturer and keynote speaker at LSE London, SMU Singapore, IFP Paris, LBMA Annual Conference in Vienna and Dubai, among others.

Diego holds a Master of Science in Mineral Economics from the Colorado School of Mines, a Master of Science in Petroleum Economics and Management from the French Institute of Petroleum in Paris, and a Master and Bachelor of Science in Mining and Petroleum Engineering at the Madrid School of Mines at the Polytechnic University of Madrid, which he completed with a full scholarship and highest academic honors.

Diego is married and the father of three children. Fluent in Spanish, English, and French, and a keen student of Mandarin Chinese, Italian, as well as foreign languages and cultures in general.

Index

OTHER TITLES IN OUR FINANCE AND FINANCIAL MANAGEMENT COLLECTION

John A. Doukas, Old Dominion University, Editor

- *Money Laundering and Terrorist Financing Activities: A Primer on Avoidance Management for Money Managers* by Milan Frankl and Ayse Ebru Kurcer
- *Introduction to Foreign Exchange Rates, Second Edition* by Thomas J. O'Brien
- *Rays of Research on Real Estate Development* by Jaime Luque
- *Weathering the Storm: The Financial Crisis and the EU Response, Volume I: Background and Origins of the Crisis* by Javier Villar Burke
- *Weathering the Storm: The Financial Crisis and the EU Response, Volume II: The Response to the Crisis* by Javier Villar Burke
- *Rethinking Risk Management: Critically Examining Old Ideas and New Concepts* by Rick Nason
- *Towards a Safer World of Banking: Bank Regulation After the Subprime Crisis* by T.T. Ram Mohan
- *Escape from the Central Bank Trap: How to Escape From the $20 Trillion Monetary Expansion Unharmed* by Daniel Lacalle
- *Tips & Tricks for Excel-Based Financial Modeling: A Must for Engineers & Financial Analysts, Volume I* by M. A. Mian
- *Tips & Tricks for Excel-Based Financial Modeling: A Must for Engineers & Financial Analysts, Volume II* by M. A. Mian

Announcing the Business Expert Press Digital Library

Concise e-books business students need for classroom and research

This book can also be purchased in an e-book collection by your library as

- a one-time purchase,
- that is owned forever,
- allows for simultaneous readers,
- has no restrictions on printing, and
- can be downloaded as PDFs from within the library community.

Our digital library collections are a great solution to beat the rising cost of textbooks. E-books can be loaded into their course management systems or onto students' e-book readers.
The **Business Expert Press** digital libraries are very affordable, with no obligation to buy in future years. For more information, please visit **www.businessexpertpress.com/librarians**. To set up a trial in the United States, please email **sales@businessexpertpress.com**.

CPSIA information can be obtained
at www.ICGtesting.com
Printed in the USA
BVHW060138010219
539152BV00006B/365/P